THE

Learning
Game

Jonathan Smith

LITTLE, BROWN AND COMPANY

A *Little, Brown* Book

First published in Great Britain in 2000
by Little, Brown and Company
Reprinted 2000 (twice)

A CIP catalogue record for this book
is available from the British Library.

ISBN 0 316 85421 2

Typeset in Bembo by M Rules
Printed and bound in Great Britain by
Clays Ltd, St Ives plc

Little, Brown and Company (UK)
Brettenham House
Lancaster Place
London WC2E 7EN

Acknowledgements

Quotation from 'Full Moon and Little Frieda' from *Wodwo* by Ted Hughes; 'This be the Verse' from *Collected Poems* by Philip Larkin; 'Fly' from *Expanded Universes* by Christopher Reid; all by kind permission of Faber and Faber Ltd. 'Walking Away' by C Day Lewis from *Complete Poems* by C Day Lewis published by Sinclair-Stevenson (1992), copyright © 1992 in this edition and the Estate of C Day Lewis. 'Sometimes' is taken from *Selected Poems* by Sheenagh Pugh (Seren, 1990). 'William Wordsworth' by Sidney Keyes from *Collected Poems of Sidney Keyes* (Routledge, 1988) by kind permission of David Higham Associates. Extracts from 'Form Photograph' (1971) by Stanley Cook by kind permission of Peterloo Poets. 'The Road Not Taken' by Robert Frost from *The Poetry of Robert Frost* by kind permission of the Estate of Robert Frost, the editor Edward Connery Lathem, and the publisher Jonathan Cape. 'Last Lesson of the Afternoon' and 'The Best of School' by D H Lawrence by kind permission of the Estate of Frieda Lawrence Ravagli and Laurence Pollinger Ltd. 'Love and Work' from *The Humble Administrator's Garden* (1985) by Vikram Seth by kind permission of Vikram Seth and Carcanet Press. Extract from *The Price* by Arthur Miller from *Miller Plays: 2* (1998, Methuen).

for Becky and Edward
– and for all my pupils

Contents

The other day I asked my colleagues if they'd ever read a good book on teaching. There was a long silence.

1
Don't Apologise

– OK, hands up, I'll come clean, I'm a teacher.
– Really?
– Yes, sorry. I came here to teach, oh . . . years ago, and here I still am.
– Still at the same school?
– Yes, still at the same school.
– Really?
– Terrible, isn't it? Sorry.
– No, that's all right . . . So, you've been at your present school all your career?
– Yes, if you leave out my early years, I suppose I have, more or less. If you can call it a career.
– But you must enjoy it, the teaching?
– Well, yes, I do, I do enjoy it. Very much.
– And to have stayed so long?
– It's flashed by, God knows where it goes, you know how it is.
– Never thought about becoming a head? Running a school?
– No.
– I'm surprised.

– Why? I came into teaching to teach.
– Never thought about moving on?
– Moving on? No, but I did think about moving out.
– Really? Giving up?
– Stepping out of the firing line, like everyone else, but I couldn't afford it. And I'm glad I didn't.
– So . . . you're still at it?
– That's it. Exactly. I'm still at it.

And while I am still at it, and without being defensive, I want to write about what it's like: while I can still feel the everyday challenge of the classroom, still feel my pulse racing and the adrenalin draining, the bustle, the battles, the conflict of egos, the frustrations and little victories, the corners turned and the bridges tentatively built. It's important to me, as a father and a teacher, to do this while I am still in touch with the young, still in touch with young teachers and still in the place where I can smell and taste the job.

But first, as a matter of interest if not of concern, why do teachers feel the need to apologise? If the British, as Martin Bell claims, can be characterised by a tendency to apologise when a stranger stands on one's foot, then the British are best represented by their teachers. Why, when I talk of my profession, am I defensive and punchy at the same time? Is it because teachers deal with the young and this suggests that we ourselves, in some important sense, have not fully grown up? That we have little status because we are not properly adult? That we do not live in the real world?

Do doctors apologise? Not when I'm around. In fact, unless we're actually dying, we tend to apologise to the doctor for taking up his time. Do solicitors, actors, engineers, architects and politicians apologise? Not that I can recall. After they've shaken your hand, I've never noticed them indulging in my quiet, shoulder-shrugging deflection when they tell you what they do for a living. They look pretty comfortable with who they are. But we teachers are always at it, and it's nothing new.

Thirty years ago, in his book *Learner Teacher* (1972), Nicholas Otty put it this way:

> People I know in other professions can make me feel singularly small and shapeless, or else foolishly missionary and dedicated, as though I had taken a morally right but socially perverse option with my life . . . People turn away from you as they do from disabled people.

Quite so.

Go back a hundred years to A.C. Benson, who was a housemaster at Eton before he became a don at Cambridge. He chose these words to begin *The Schoolmaster* (1902):

> I think it must be conceded at the outset that there clings about the profession of schoolmastering a certain slight social disability. It is not a profession which, to use a vile phrase, 'leads to' anything in particular.

Indeed, in Benson's time in the classroom in the 1890s, some teachers were so embarrassed by their way of earning a living that they went even further than apologise. They were in denial.

> A master of my acquaintance, who was keenly alive to the social disabilities of his trade, was reduced to saying to his fashionable friends who asked him what he had been doing, that he had been staying in Bedfordshire.

We may smile at that, but even a hundred years later it is still the case. Even today, many teacher-writers and teacher-musicians, i.e. those who earn their daily bread from teaching but who also have a second career in writing or music, are still in denial. They want to be known only as writers or musicians. To this end they will snobbishly delete their teaching lives from their dust jackets and programme notes. Basically it is too shaming. This drab admission will do their more glamorous second career no good. They beg their media friends not to mention it. Indeed I have often been told not only to change my name (too ordinary) but also to delete my teaching career at an independent school from the dust jacket (it will work against you).

At a dinner party given in 1983 by a successful lawyer, now a judge, I told the guests on either side of me at the table that I was a teacher – no doubt accompanying the confession with the appropriately apologetic body language. Both were women, and one of them was beautiful and sexy (even a teacher could spot it), but she was much more interested in the man on her right. She turned her back on me and her eyes on him. Now, I hate to judge a man one along at dinner too quickly, but even at that distance I could see . . . Still, that was the way her beautiful neck was turned, and no doubt he was a banker or lawyer or doctor or politician.

At secondary level, the level at which I teach, teachers spend their time teaching (try not to state the obvious), caring for and trying (usually successfully) to control teenagers. That is a tough and very interesting job. Schools are dynamic and human places. Parents who are finding it very stressful living with their adolescent daughters and sons – we can all swap horror stories – should sometimes reflect that teachers have their classrooms full of adolescents every day, all day.

That being the case, presumably the teachers have picked up something along the way, perhaps even something about life. Teachers and parents have, it seems to me, a vast amount to say to each other not only about the individual child, about your child, but about bringing up and handling children of all ages. You might even argue that what teachers say about the individual child or your child or children in general should be taken seriously. At the very least, whether at parents' evenings or in the pub or on the telephone or (as in this instance) at a dinner party, it's good to talk . . . But she was looking away.

Later in the meal, an old friend sitting opposite me asked me what I thought about the latest episode of the current TV drama serial. Did I approve?

'Quite,' I said, wrinkling my nose. I sort of did, sort of didn't.

'Don't you wish you'd adapted it?'

'Of course I do,' I said. 'I'd have made more money.'

'What's it like seeing a book you've written mucked around by some hack?'

'He's not a hack.'

'Even so.'

'OK, I think I'd have done a better job,' I said, 'but I'm still very glad it's happened.'

'And you must be pleased. This week's *Radio Times*? Front cover!'

The woman on my right, the woman I had spotted was sexy, was now stirring. She quickly disengaged herself from the Boring Bloke on her right.

'Which TV serial is that?' she asked my friend.

'The one they've made out of Jonathan's novel. Surely you're . . .'

And now she looked at me.

'You mean *you* wrote that?'

Look, I don't want to make too much out of this, not with the photo you can see on the cover of this book, but you'll just have to believe me: she really looked at me. She looked at me in an entirely different way. Even a teacher, unused to the wiles of The Real World, could see the difference. You know the big poster of Paul Newman in his late thirties, with his

steady, amused mouth and his cornflower-blue eyes, the one
some of my ex-girlfriends used to pin up in their loos just to
remind you what a really good-looking guy looked like? Well,
I'm not for one moment saying that at the dinner table that
night I was Paul Newman, but for a brief second I certainly
was no ordinary schoolteacher.

Why? Because I had been blessed by TV. I'd had a novel
serialised on TV. My novel was now not just a novel, not just
any novel, no longer just a good read, no longer even the
same book, because IT HAD BEEN ON TV. You have to put
that kind of achievement in capital letters or else in italics, as
Wordsworth does in *The Prelude*, when he finds, without realising it, that he has crossed the Alps. He looks at the
mountains, he checks his map, he questions a peasant again
and again, and indeed it was true that

we had crossed the Alps

– and it was equally true that

I had a novel on TV.

I wasn't just a teacher. Now I could hold my head up in any
company.

2
Talk To Babies In Prams

The father who never says more than 'Hullo' to his son and goes out to the nearest bar every evening is teaching the boy as emphatically as though he were standing over him with a strap. It's a very tricky business, teaching.

GILBERT HIGHET, *The Art of Teaching* (1950)

When you talk about teaching it is difficult not to sound as if you are stating the obvious. Because . . . well, you are. And yet it is obviousness of a tricky kind. I feel exactly the same in the classroom when I am teaching Wordsworth, one of our greatest poets and teachers: his poetry is at once both very simple and yet very demanding. You introduce it and read it and talk about it, and it is clearly so important and central to our lives, yet on one level it almost invites a 'So what? So what are you going to *say* about it?'

Even so, I want to keep clear of jargon and to shy away from education-speak, because such language is usually no more than an attempt to make the superficial sound profound. Obscurity, as W. H. Auden reminds us, is mostly swank, and a lot of swank passes for intellectual life.

In much the same way, it is difficult to talk about being a parent without sounding pompous or confessional. Nobody likes know-alls, and few children like those cringingly inappropriate heart-to-hearts when a parent spills the beans about his past. Nevertheless, in writing this book, I have seen myself as a father writing for parents as much as a teacher writing for those interested in education. While thinking about my classes my mind has often been on my own children as children and as pupils. Indeed, whenever I think about education, in the concrete or the abstract, the two roles I play, teacher and father – and there's a great deal of play-acting in both – are so close together in my mind that they become the same concern.

There is no doubt that I approached my job differently once I became a father. The change happened slowly. It was not thought out or conscious, but I sensed it in my hands and in my voice and in my response. In the classroom I became more willing to listen, more forgiving and understanding, perhaps even a bit more of a soft touch, yet also more sharply aware of a pupil's strategies and manipulative skills. What I was learning from my life with my children at home I took to my pupils at school, and vice-versa.

In a natural way I saw, and in a sense still do see, each pupil as potentially one of my own children, not so much (I hope) as a Mr Chips but embracing the feeling that being a father has made me both react differently and grow as a teacher. My children, too, as they went through their school years, were a daily reminder of the pressure schoolchildren are under, of what they are expected to do in and out of class, and a daily reminder of how unreasonable or barking mad or inflexible or inadequate much of the work set them was.

Not only did I see at first hand the pressures from both sides of the desk but I learnt from my children's response to those demands and expectations. To their intense frustration, when they wanted me to take sides in a dispute, I always backed the school. They said that was unfair and, given the evidence, unintelligent. I told them life was unfair. They encouraged me to make life, in this particular instance, a little less unfair. I told them to shut up and get on with it. They told me that reaction was unworthy of me. I can't remember my next move. Probably towards the drinks cupboard.

As Gilbert Highet points out, albeit a little too worthily, at the beginning of this chapter, all parents teach by example. Consciously or otherwise, for good or ill, through sins of omission and commission, all parents teach their children. You can't help it. From day one of their lives, from the first day of every school year, children are watching us, imitating us, just as pupils watch and mimic a teacher. One of the skills most rehearsed and practised in a school is taking off the teacher. I have often been in buses and theatres and swung round, surprised to think I had an unexpected colleague along with me, only to see a pupil embodying a perfect imitation. One boy I produced recently in a play could 'do' the whole staff in a performance which challenged Rory Bremner. The only take-off you tend not to spot is the one of you. Which is worrying.

Children and pupils see much more of us and in us and about us than we would like to imagine. They study us as they study their books, and often with considerably more interest. They read us. They see our body language and see through it; they spot where we scratch ourselves; they pick up the giveaway expressions in our eyes; they work out our values and smile at our evasions; they perceive our natures and assess our flash-points. No actor on the stage is more carefully studied. (The more I roll on with this rather rhetorical paragraph the more anxious I am beginning to feel.)

Beyond loving them, the best that we can do for our children is to make them interested, interested in things, in the hope that this will make them interesting. Whenever I think about the connection between love and interest I always see that 1980s car window sticker: 'Have You Hugged Your Kid Today?' No one on this side of the Atlantic can read that car sticker without an ironic smile or a guilty wince or a sick-making gesture. It smacks so much of American openness, warmth and public sentimentality. They work on hugging their kids, the Americans, they work on it. As to whether that is a good or a bad thing, I would give a different answer on different days.

Well, 'Yes!' I want to shout. 'Yes, I have hugged my kid today and mind your own business. Who the hell are you to tell me how to express my affection? And may I ask you a question back, if you're not rushing off? Uh, excuse me? Have you *talked* to your kid today? Because talking and listening takes longer than hugging and is often more loving. Hugging's the easy bit. Some of the most insincere people I know are serial huggers.'

However busy and preoccupied we are, nothing beats a seriously good and demanding chat with your pupils or with your child, a real exchange of views and feelings, even if it sometimes turns into an argument or, as it is prone to do at home, descends into a row.

There is, of course, a considerable cross-over between an early influence outside the schoolroom – and who better for this than a parent? – and the early school experience. I still love watching parents collect their children from the primary school in Tonbridge where my children went (a school so like the one both my parents taught at) and hearing the children talking about what happened in their day in the classroom and playground. There is so much energy, lively concern, vivid retelling and eye-contact. Keep talking, that's it, keep talking, I want to say to them (but wouldn't for fear of an arrest), keep talking: fluency before facts, rephrasing before know-how, articulacy before getting the answers right.

I have two children, by the way, a girl and a boy. To ensure the Smith family kept to its tradition of educational tension, one went on to a state secondary school and one to an independent school.

'No prizes for who went to which!' my daughter shouts.

'I'll talk about that later.'

Although my wife spent more time with our children than I did, I want here to grapple only with what I was trying to do. From the very first I wanted them to enjoy words. No surprises there: I read English at university, I teach English, I love talking, I love radio, and I write fiction and plays. From the very first day of their lives I spoke to them as much as I could. I was encouraged to do this by a nurse at our doctor's and it was the best advice I have ever been given. Lots of fathers, I know, leave home too early in the morning and come back too late to do this, but the advice still holds good.

In 1974, the year we lived in Australia, Rebecca went from three months old to fifteen months. Whenever I came in from school I would wheel her round the Melbourne suburbs in her pram, and talk to her. She was very attentive, her eyes rarely leaving my face. Sometimes I got strange looks from the people I passed because very few men in 1974 in Australia walked prams on their own (I couldn't care less about that, then or now) and because I was talking intelligently to a baby in a pram, talking as if I were conversing with an adult. Whatever kind of day I'd had, I told her everything, sometimes getting all my professional frustrations off my chest. I gave her my perceptions about Australia and my new Australian friends, comparing our two countries, describing the new fiction and poetry I was reading, as well as the joys and problems I was facing as a teacher and as a sports coach. I asked her rhetorical questions. Sometimes I used two or three voices in an improvised dialogue, playing verbal games with myself, and watched her laugh. Looking at her face as I pounded the pavements I felt a lot was going on and going in. As a teacher, look at their eyes to see if they're grasping it.

By the time I arrived home I had walked five or six miles, given my wife a break, was feeling a virtuous father, and was morally more than ready for a serious drink. Before putting her to bed my wife read aloud from *Winnie the Pooh* and danced her around and played music. The talking and the reading and the rhythms would, I hoped, seamlessly join.

When Becky started to talk herself I listened, of course I listened (listened? I loved it!), as all parents do, thrilled as each word framed in her mind and shaped on her tongue and landed in our lives. Ted Hughes captures that pride perfectly when he describes his daughter 'Little Frieda' saying 'Moon! Moon!':

> *Cows are going home in the lane there, looping the hedges*
> > *with their warm wreaths of breath –*
> *A dark river of blood, many boulders,*
> *Balancing unspilt milk.*
>
> *'Moon!' you cry suddenly, 'Moon! Moon!'*
> *The moon has stepped back like an artist gazing*
> > *amazed at a work*
> *That points at him amazed.*

With my son, Edward, a few years later, it was the same, exactly the same as with Becky, talk and listen, listen and talk, except he had an extra teacher to contend with, and the strictest of the lot: his sister. When she came in from school she set up her own classroom and sat him down in the front row. There was no mucking about. This was one-on-one Victorian teaching of the most rigorous kind. Every now and then I popped in to find out how it was all going and to check the birch wasn't out.

To see my pupils – or to see my children – realise how vivid a word is, how it can hit or be relished, how it can be applied like a splodge of paint or glance away like a ripple, to see them enjoy both the sound and the form of a word, to create in them a sense of wonder, the infinite possibilities of words rather than their reductibility – that's what I was after when my children were young and that's what I'm still after every day in my classes. I see words as a way to draw the young out of any possibility of passivity. They can practise intellectual shots, practise sentences, hear the rise and fall of a sentence, just as they can practise a dance step, do a somersault or watch the rise and fall of a ball into the hand.

Of course there were huge areas of which, as a father, I knew nothing and still do know nothing, e.g. science, mathematics, other languages, computers. I am hopelessly uneducated in so many ways and not one bit proud of it. I enjoy watching friends and teachers introducing their young to so much of the world which is more or less closed to me. My wider point is: does it matter much on what one focuses, as long as it encourages concentration, absorption and a sense of wonder?

Just as important to me was for my children to develop sensitivity to emotion. I have arrived at most of my conclusions in life through feeling and through experience rather than through sustained thought. Love of words, yes, habits of enquiry, yes, hours of application, yes, but it all had to go hand in hand with the human dimension: it needed heart. I wanted my children to feel the concerns of the heart just as much as I wanted them to cut to the heart of the matter. There was little point, I felt, in developing the critical sense, in examining life, in deploying a persuasive mind unless that mind was warm. Clever, 'care-less' people are to me among the most loathsome.

Music, acting, sport, film, we talked and practised and analysed. Even at the end of a teacher's day, when there wasn't much tether left and what tether there was did not seem best attuned to the young, I tried to be patient and considerate. Impossible goals. As was tolerance, which for a while I gave a capital T, treating it almost as a god-word. There is a myth of tolerance amongst some teachers. I bought the myth and became too tolerant with my children and with my pupils. I allowed too much. It's an easy and tempting path because it is close to loving, but you need to keep an edge of intolerance, a sense that there's a line. As you get older that line can move in the sand, move to the point where you start to think that not only the line but the very sand itself is shifting.

At home occasionally I snapped. Then my wife and I would regroup and try to win back some territory. As a family we argued, and the more skilful my children became with words the more difficult it was for me to be a father. 'You sort them out,' I said to myself. 'Be a father!' But I'd taught them how to punch and, by God, they punched. They took the keys, raided the armoury and came out all guns blazing. My early pride and pleasure was now mixed with increasing annoyance and a developing sense of powerlessness. In modern jargon (permit me just one) I had well and truly empowered them.

'Your fault,' they used to laugh. 'Don't blame us.'

By the time they had finished with me I was no longer a good listener. All my tolerance theories were in tatters. Head down, towel thrown in, I sat in the corner of the ring, punch-drunk.

Do parents want power over their children? Some, yes, undoubtedly do. And as their children grow, parents often find their own position and authority eroded. Some teachers go into the profession to exert this kind of psycho-sexual power; these teachers often strike me as frustrated prefects, acting out in their adult lives the dominant roles denied them in their own schooldays.

Some parents, equally, never let go. They always set the agenda and firmly exert their domination until the end of their lives. Some even continue to do so from beyond the grave. I wanted my children to have the questioning strength that words give, the strength of an independent mind and the capacity to look after themselves. I wanted them to know the priceless gift of a language enjoyed and exercised at the highest levels, the gift which sharpens the cutting edge – or *is* the cutting edge.

At times I have almost regretted it because that part of their lives could seem out of kilter with the rest of their developing personalities. What came out of their mouths was racing ahead of the game and invited accusations of arrogance. They seemed too verbal, to press too hard. On many occasions as a parent there is only so much of that one can take. An infinite stock of patience is unreal. In class, too, the atmosphere can quickly deteriorate, to the disadvantage of the majority, if one pupil simply won't accept that only so much time can be given up to exploring his controversial, or more likely boring, idea. At home, as my children grew in confidence, I could feel I was being challenged too relentlessly to define and to redefine a point. Equally, the criticism that I had over-encouraged such verbal sophistication could be laid at my door as a father – and it has been.

Certainly in her last two years at primary school Becky went through a language crisis. She became unhappy and started to pull her hair out, strand by strand at first, until there was a large thinning patch down the middle of her scalp. During this unhappy phase she found out that she got on much better with the other girls if she stopped using long words, if she collected marbles instead of using words like mundane. If she stopped using a wide vocabulary and started collecting marbles, they stopped calling her posh. Simple. So she stopped using a wide vocabulary. Suddenly they were all asking her to tea. She gave away her best marbles to her new friends. Now she was popular. She learnt about not only collecting marbles but collecting stickers and rubbers and running fast across the playground. She had dumbed down.

Even so, articulation is what I had to offer my daughter and son, and it is what I offer to other parents. Nothing, of course, replaces or can ever replace good, formal schooling. No family can match what a good school can offer, and would be very pushed to outstrip even a moderate school. As you will discover, I am a great believer in organised, disciplined and flexible education: not de-schooled, then, but well-schooled. Most schools that have thrown out organised, disciplined and flexible education aren't here to tell the tale. They died the death.

But you can achieve so much more with a child in school if that child has been taught from the very first day of its life by loving and interested parents. It starts, day one. That underpins everything. Even those people who might consider themselves too good for a career in teaching would surely see the virtue of teaching their own children.

3

Bad Low Toad

A letter from Kenneth Grahame to his daughter.

Green Bank Hotel,
Falmouth
10th May 1907

My Darling Mouse,

Have you heard about Toad? He was never taken prisoner by brigands at all. It was all a horrid low trick of his. He wrote that letter himself – the letter saying that a hundred pounds must be put in the hollow tree. And he got out of the window early one morning, & went off to a town called Buggleton, & went to the Red Lion Hotel & there he found a party that had just motored down from London, & while they were having breakfast he went into the stable-yard & found their motor-car & went off in it without even saying Poop-poop! And now he has vanished & every one is looking for him, including the police. I fear he is a bad low animal.

Goodbye, from
Your loving Daddy.

4

Winston Churchill Writes To His Dearest Father

8th October 1887

Dearest Father,

I am very glad to hear that I am going to Harrow and not to Winchester. I think I shall pass the Entrance Examination, which is not so hard as Winchester . . . Did you go to Eton or Harrow? I should like to know. Please do not forget the autographs.

with love and kisses I remain, your loving son,

Winston S. Churchill

5
Uncle Bert

My father did not talk to me in my pram. Even if he had wanted to do so, which is open to doubt, it would have been impossible because for the formative years of my life he was away in the war. Indeed I hardly saw him for my first four years. In the year I was born, 1942 – the year (I think we can all agree on this) in which the tide turned and we started to win the war – we moved out from Gloucester city, which was being badly bombed, to rural Gloucestershire: in fact to a small village near Berkeley, famous for its Berkeley Castle, infamous as the Berkeley Castle in which Edward II met his brutal end, an end my father often alluded to but could never quite bring himself to describe. With my father away working on radar with Bomber Command, my mother returned with us to the family home to look after her widowed father and one of her brothers, my Uncle Bert.

Uncle Bert, though a fiercely independent and proud man, needed some looking after because he was a haemophiliac. For those who do not know, haemophilia is a rare condition in which the blood fails to clot after injury due to a deficiency of factor VIII, one of a number of proteins involved in the clotting reaction. This condition is determined by a recessive gene and is sex-linked, in the sense that only females carry the gene and only males are affected. It was once common enough in the royal families of Europe but it also – as is clear from our case – afflicted more modest people. The treatment of haemophilia has improved dramatically in the last fifty years, but for the seven years I was living with Uncle Bert it was life-threatening. So when I say or write the sentence 'Teaching is in my blood' I can't help thinking of Uncle Bert. Our family's blood was a permanent anxiety.

Teaching is in my blood. On a deeper level, too, the sentence is entirely appropriate because Uncle Bert was my first inspiration and my first teacher. At any stage of the year he could be laid up in bed, sometimes for months on end. If he was laid up I sat on the end of his bed, being very careful not to bang into or bump him, and he talked to me. He talked to me about everything. He asked me questions on everything; he engaged my mind.

Any small injury to him was a crisis. Clipping his knee on the corner of the kitchen table, which for most of us would call for no more than an 'Ouch!' and a quick rub, was a crisis. His whole leg would go as blue-black as a stormy sky. He was always vulnerable to these debilitating and dangerous bleeds, sometimes being rushed to hospital: I hated watching him being carried out of the front door. To cut himself shaving was a daily risk, though once he had finished shaving (a ritual I loved watching) his face was as red and shiny as the Worcester apples on the trees at the bottom of the garden. When battery razors came in there was great relief in the family and around his bed, though I did miss the smell of his shaving soap, his enamel mug full of steaming water and the feel on my cheek of his bristly brush. Grinning mischievously, he would sometimes cover my face in the warm foam and say, 'The day will surely come.' His bed, the centre of my childhood, was set up high, allowing him to sit on it without having to bend too much. He had a 'made-up' shoe, a wheelchair, an airgun and some chickens. He shot the rats and threw grain to the chickens.

More important for my education, Uncle Bert clearly Had Time for me – which is what the young most need from their parents and from their teachers – and he most certainly Had Views. In his ill health he was my daily companion. His great misfortune with his blood was a great benefaction to me: it is indeed 'an ill wind'. He talked to me, he challenged me, and he wickedly teased me. When my brother and I had been playing hide and seek in the garden for hours on end and I had become quite frantic with frustration because there was *nowhere left he could be* and he wasn't even up the may tree and he was *nowhere*, Uncle Bert secretly waved me to come closer to his wheelchair. He bent down and made me promise never ever to let on to my brother that he'd told me but – he whispered and helpfully flicked his eyes and pointed – if I looked in the teapot I would find him hiding in there. I tiptoed over and whipped off the top . . .

In my early years he talked to me about God, right and wrong, the Bible, suffering, politics, communism, government, doctors, good people and bad people in the village, and about animals who knew far more than we humans often thought. He was opinionated, irascible, quick to be kind himself and easily cantankerous. He loved to laugh and he was, not surprisingly, often depressed. He loved a challenging exchange, a good disagreement, and above all he enjoyed having the last word. Indeed he always saw that he got it. We all left his bedroom to a Parthian shot.

How lucky I was in my first teacher. Uncle Bert told you things, which is what teachers should do (and increasingly do not); he was 'there' for me, lying or sitting on his bed, until I was seven (when my father was made a headmaster of a primary school and we moved down the A38 to a north Bristol

suburb). On one of Uncle Bert's good days my brother and I
sometimes pushed him round the lanes in his wheelchair. By
turns witty and stern, he pointed out things in nature that we
might miss.

Though not a professionally trained teacher, like his sisters
and brothers-in-law, Uncle Bert was a natural, a man who
was interested in everything himself and wanted to transfer
that interest to the young. He saw me, I believe, as a pupil as
well as his nephew. He saw me first as blotting paper, then as
a sounding board and finally as a person with a tongue and a
mind of his own. His bed was his classroom, his garden and
the lanes around Berkeley were his Lake District, and like
Wordsworth, he was my guide and mentor.

Because he had not spent much time in work (as a young
man he was briefly a clerk on the railways) he was idealistic
and, I suppose, unworldly. As a result, he did not offer you
compromises or grey areas. He told the truth, which could
often make him uncomfortable company, as most of us tell
lies some of the time and often far more than we like to
admit even to ourselves. He was, as my Aunty Joan always
said, as straight as a die.

He told me the Parables. He had read the Bible, every
word of it, twice. I know this as a fact because he did not lie
and he told me he had read it twice – not skim reading, real
reading, go-on-then-and-ask-me-about-it reading. Many
people claim to have read the Bible. Many people claim to
have read Spenser. Many people claim to have read Salman
Rushdie. Ask most of those who claim to have read the Bible
or Spenser or Salman Rushdie to tell you anything in detail
about the Bible or Spenser or Salman Rushdie and I find
they're usually off looking for another drink.

In his book *The Philosophy of Teaching* (1980), John
Passmore describes the many faces of the modern English
teacher in the following way:

The English teacher is commonly expected to inculcate certain habits of a formal kind, as well as certain intellectual habits . . . he is expected to train certain capacities . . . he is expected to encourage such of his pupils as exhibit an inclination to be writers; he is expected to cultivate in his pupils a particular form of critical attitude, a capacity to distinguish the good from the pretentious . . . he is expected to arouse in them a particular form of enthusiasm . . . He is held responsible for their personal development and social competence . . . Not surprisingly he is often overwhelmed by the magnitude of his task.

Much of that rings true, and many of those Protean expectations – particularly on the moral and social side – began for me with the example of my uncle.

Take personal development and social competence. He had haemophilia. I, as a male in the family, could have been similarly afflicted, but was not. Without making a meal of it, listening to and watching Uncle Bert introduced me to, and made me think about, the random cruelty and injustice of life. Fate had dealt him a rotten hand (which he never mentioned) but he did tell me that 'Handicapped people are usually shunned.' He said it was a natural reaction but it could be easily overcome. Decency and good manners required you to overcome your instinctive reaction; thinking of the spirit of the person within that disabled body ensured you did. People, in his view, either looked away or moved away from the disabled not from unkindness but from embarrassment. When, some years later, he had a battery-driven chair and used to travel around the district to watch local football matches he noticed that the other spectators always drifted away from the place on the touchline where he stopped to watch. There was the same problem in nature, he said: on our walks around the lanes he pointed out that the other animals always left the odd one in the corner of the field. He told me never to feel superior but to say what I saw, to read, to be brave (if I could), to climb trees, to be fearless in my questioning and to face unpalatable truths. He suggested I read the Bible but did not bother about the Church.

Whenever I teach Greek tragedy or Shakespearean tragedy or Webster or Ibsen or Hardy I see his face and I hear his voice. And that stops me talking comfortable claptrap. Uncle Bert always denied that pain and suffering could be ennobling. 'Pain hurts,' he said. 'You want it to stop. That is all.' ('Philosophy is one thing,' wrote Machado de Assis, the Brazilian novelist, 'and actual dying is another.') Whether witnessing how others deal with their pain and suffering can be inspiring and ennobling is, of course, another matter, and when reading tragic literature we can perhaps learn by suffering vicariously with the victim-heroes. Just as certainly as I first stretched my mind and often laughed myself silly in his company, I also learnt about suffering from my uncle.

Indeed, I will never understand how he could take so much for so long. He saw the question in my eyes when I was a middle-aged man and he was near the end. 'You have to,' he said. 'You have no choice.' Thinking of him as a man and as a teaching example still inspires me. Whenever I am exhausted from teaching or finding writing difficult or things aren't going too well in my life and I'm slipping into self-pity, I only have to say his name out loud on a walk to start climbing back.

One last anecdote, if I may, about Uncle Bert and you will perhaps see how his insight into his young nephew, as well as his humour and skill in handling him, may have subtly influenced a little boy to become a teacher.

Every Christmas Day for many years we all gathered in his room for our dinner. After dinner, in my early childhood, we always played cards. I looked forward to this as much as to the turkey because I concentrated so fiercely and I wanted to win. The grown-ups gradually lost interest in the game and drank cider, with only half a mind on the cards. Taking full advantage of that, I usually ended up with the biggest pile of coins, and as the pile grew I pictured the fountain pen I was going to buy. A Platignum pen, or at least I think that's what it was called. Anyway, I had seen them in the shops. Uncle Bert, impressed by my judgement and my memory for the cards, egged me on. I massacred everyone, and 'By God, I was rich. Rich!'

By bedtime I had scooped the pool. As well as my Christmas presents the Platignum pen was as good as in my hand. Uncle Bert then reached up with his long fingers to unhook the Haemophiliac Society Charity stocking which he always kept hanging by his bed. He passed it round, encouraging each of us to contribute. It was a small see-through stocking, so there was no disguising the size of your gift. It may have been easy being mean with the collection bag in church, but not here in his bedroom. He watched me intently across the table and I knew he was watching me. One bushy eyebrow raised, a big grin and his few teeth showing, he handed the stocking to me. With a sinking heart I dropped coin after coin in.

'It's very good of you,' he said, nodding each coin down, flicking his eyes and his head back to my pile, watching it diminish, 'very good of you indeed.'

That is a teacher at work: mischief on the moral high ground, coercion, charity and comeuppance: sometimes he was pure Dickens.

As well as having no husband on hand, and my brother and me and Uncle Bert to look after, my mother sometimes complained she had my grandfather to contend with. My grandfather, a powerful railwayman, worked hard and he drank hard and there were three pubs – The Prince of Wales, The Star and the White Hart – to pass on his way from the station to his home. (Uncle Bert told me there were three kinds of drinkers, those who got nice when they drank, those who got nasty, and those who suddenly slid from nice to nasty. Right again.)

Sometimes, when patience in the kitchen was running thin at the weekend, I was sent down to the local to get Grandad back. In fact I used to offer to go down there: in a sense I was already in unspoken league with my grandfather because he knew I knew where he kept his screw-top flagons of beer hidden. He hid them in the straw at the back of the summer-house. This was his tactic, so that if ever he was under pressure to refrain and was forced to grumble, 'All right then, I *won't* go down the pub', he still had a drink ready on tap. Grandad told me not to mention it and I never did. So when I arrived at the window of the pub and pointed up to the house, he liked to call me in and say to the landlord, 'Doesn't miss much, mind, this little bugger.'

Once I had worked it out, I liked the sound of that rough praise. Anyway, if it was true that I didn't miss much, what was it like, my first school, the place where I had my first formal instruction and my first opportunity to see my family's profession in action? (Although, at different times, my mother, my father and one of my aunties all taught at Berkeley County Primary, it was not until my Bristol primary school that I encountered my family face to face in the classroom. I'll come back to that.)

Let me reconstruct a day in a rural primary school straight after the Second World War. My first day was in January 1947, I had just turned five, and it was one of the worst winters this century. That January everywhere was freezing and by February most of the country was snowbound. To make it even worse we still had no electricity or running water in my grandfather's home and the kitchen range often refused to light up. Because we lived just under two miles from Berkeley School we did not qualify for a bus ride so, well muffled, my brother and I walked.

What did I find? The building – still there, though now an hotel and restaurant – had a wide frontage, with many steps leading up to the entrance, the steps stretching across the full width of the school. In the winter, especially that winter, they were very slippy and dangerous. On my second day I fell and cut my eyebrow and still sport the scar. The classroom windows were tall and elegant with arched tops and wide stone sills, resembling the church which was close to the back of the school.

Go through the front door and you came to three interconnecting classrooms, all heated by large tortoiseshell stoves. These stoves were well protected by tall fire guards against which the teachers warmed their bottoms, sometimes lifting their skirts. In a very cold spell, such as that one, the crates of milk delivered by the local farmer were also put round the stove, the milk tasting even more disgusting when lukewarm. Given the choice, give me frozen lumps. Even thinking of lukewarm school milk still makes me feel bilious. Bilious, don't ask me why, was a big word in my childhood, people were always being bilious, sometimes 'as bilious as a Bengal general'.

The rooms led, one to another, to the Infants' Department where, as a five-year-old, I started that January on a life which has since largely been spent in classrooms. From the infants' room you stepped out on to the walled school yard, to a world of skipping ropes and hoops and to games of hopscotch and 'Oranges and Lemons', and to a row of primitive lavatories which were simply one or two holes surrounded by wooden boards. The lavatory paper was neatly cut-up squares of old newspapers hanging on strings. Also hanging around was a very strong carbolic smell.

About twenty of us were in the Infants, split into three groups: the newcomers (the five-year-olds, including me), the six-year-olds and the seven-year-olds. Three classes in one, a real challenge for any teacher's discipline, and based I suppose on the idea (or the hope) that the youngest children would learn a good deal from the older ones.

Reading was taught through the alphabet, through seeing the shapes and through listening to the sounds, e.g.

> a . . . and a nicely drawn apple that looked like an a (I liked the apples in the garden)
>
> b . . . a bat and a ball (I liked cricket; my handsome Uncle Derek played cricket)
>
> c . . . a cat curled up in a c shape (never so sure about cats)
>
> c.a.t.? c . . . a . . . t . . . spells 'cat', children, look at the cat! (cue cat noises)

Each classroom had a cumbersome easel and board from which we copied all this on to our slates.

Our fingers were essential in the teaching of numbers, in learning the clear-cut issues of arithmetic, fingers up, fingers down, one hand, two hands, no, both hands up I said, one hand and one finger equals six, hold up both hands and take away two fingers and what have you got? Nine. Which silly boy said nine? We also used the abacus, sliding the coloured balls up and down the wires, and abacus, children, is one of the very first words in the dictionary because it starts with . . . come on, it starts with? . . . a, yes, a, then comes? . . . b . . . ab . . . AB (I looked it up at home and abacus came just after aardvark and Aaron).

All our times-tables were, of course, chanted, and that bit I loved, the boys in particular shouting out louder and louder, all building up to bawling out the climaxes, 'Twelve twelves are a hun-dred and FOR-TY FOUR!', the whole class shouting in triumph. Ten years later all this was scorned as very bad teaching.

Each morning we wrote out the alphabet, row after row, on to our slates, then wiped the slates clean with the scraps of material which the teacher handed out. Pencils and lined paper were luxuries only introduced after the Infants, when you went upstairs at eight to join the top class, taught by the headmaster. My brother was already up there, learning the 'essentials', working for the scholarship (the 11-plus), getting up the headmaster's nose and slipping a ruler down the test questions to keep his mind from wandering.

Mind you, my brother's mind, a very sharp instrument, did wander. He was lively, my older brother, a quick-witted ginger-haired boy with a straight look and a gift for subversive literalness. 'Right,' the headmaster said, 'I'm going to tell you a story and if anyone does not want to sit quietly and listen to this story he can go out now.' Before he could get much beyond 'Once upon a time . . .' brother David was straight out and across the road to play in the conker field, collecting a smack on the ear on the way.

As well as telling wonderful stories to all the classes – most children, like most readers of adult fiction, like to be hooked and brought to heel and driven on by narrative – the headmaster, Mr Edmonds, played the piano with his back to it, looking not at the keys but at the pupils, a feat I've not seen done since. He did not do this because he was afraid of anyone flicking paper or throwing bits of clay; he did it to show off, and we loved it. Teachers are actors. Teachers need a performing personality. Control, I could already see, was part of the act, and the act was part and parcel of the personality.

We all sang nursery rhymes and the more extrovert pupils, usually the girls, stood up to make the appropriate actions

and to enjoy the physical interpretation. A favourite in 1947
was 'I'm a Little Tea-pot':

I'm a little tea-pot
short and stout

here is my handle   *(one hand on hip for handle)*
here is my spout   *(bent arm on other side for spout)*

when I get my steam up
hear me shout

tip me over
And – *pour* me out!   *(whole body tips over to whole class
                            making gushing sound)*

In a large cupboard behind her desk Miss, the teacher, kept
her 'make-up clothes'. These were for acting any part if you
wanted to make up a story – and it was here that my belief in
the importance of acting began. The annual use of the
clothes, of course, was for Joseph and Mary and the angels, but
much more interesting was the way our make-up moments
revealed our natures, the way in which we fell into our selves:
you could see the bully, the shy, the jumpy, the 'big head', the
quick to cry, the mummy's boy, the catapultist, the tongue-
tied, the unhappy, it all came out. Far from covering up the
truth, 'make up' more often exposes a raw human face. For a
teacher these are priceless moments. During these infant revelations, which were much less clear-cut than arithmetic, I
learnt to listen and I learnt to watch.
   Every now and then, in an early morning raid much more
frightening than any Germans, the nurses landed like para-
chutists for their room-to-room nit search. There was no
hiding place. We were all lined up. They walked along the

rows of different-coloured heads and peered down on to your
scalp. I was itching long before they got to me. No secrets, no
hiding place, and we would all soon find out who the 'dirty'
children were, and after the nurses left we slid our chairs a
little further away from the dirty ones, uugghh, who'd picked
up the nits. (Worms were another worry, involving much
peering down the lavatory, but at least we weren't all lined up
for that one.)

The cane was used but not very often. Usually it was a tap
over the knuckles with a ruler or a sharp slap with the hand
behind the knees or you were sent outside. I was never sent
outside at Berkeley though I was once tied up with a rope
inside, tied literally (but not tightly) to the central pillar
that went from the classroom floor to the ceiling. I was tied
up for an hour for being rude. Miss asked us all what the
most important part of your body was, expecting 'head' or
'heart', but I offered the unacceptable member I was holding
on to. The answer, I still maintain, depends on your point of
view.

Every afternoon the youngest of us had a rest for half an
hour. Some went fast asleep but I never did. You had to fold
your arms neatly and put your head on the desk, while the
older ones tip-toed noisily around Miss. Miss often took this
opportunity to knit some socks or to make up (that word
again) her face in her small powder compact mirror. My eyes
(over fifty years ago) explored these silent receptive moments,
much as they still do now when I take the chance to look
around my classes as they enjoy their silent afternoon reading
lesson. There's often more human interest in a silent classroom moment than in noisily extrovert ones.

So, what did I learn from my first primary school? I think I
learnt these things: to value memory, to value repetition, to
respect clarity in an explanation, to be wary of angry eyes and
clouded brows, to enjoy make-believe, to humour lunatics, to

avoid bullies and, above all, to listen and to watch. As a
potential teacher – though of course I did not know it then,
let alone think in the terms I am now writing – I was on the
way, on the way to knowing that a teacher's ready smile
achieved more control and discipline than shouting 'No! No!
No! Wrong! Wrong! Wrong!', and that for a class to work it
needed to be held together by a teacher's special presence.

Because I was often unwell I missed many months of
schooling in my first two years, but even then I was a lucky
boy. Uncle Bert was always there, always back at home,
padding slowly around or sitting in the garden or waiting for
me to go up to his room and tell him things or even, a special
treat, coming to my room to sit on *my* bed. He was always kind
when I was ill, but never less than intellectually testing.

6
The Real World

– So, you're a teacher.
– That's right.
– Like your father and mother.
– And my Aunty Eva.
– She was a teacher too?
– And my Aunty Joan.
– It runs in the family, then?
– And Uncle Bill. And Uncle Will.
– And all this didn't put you off?
– And when I got married, my father-in-law was a teacher. And my brother-in-law. And my sister-in-law. And my wife, of course.
– Was anyone not a teacher?
– A few. They made the money.
– And all teaching in state schools?
– All except me.
– Did that cause any problems? Any frictions?
– You mean philosophically? Between us?
– Yes.
– You mean that I'd taken the easy route? That I'd sold out? That I was a class traitor? That teaching in an

all-boys school in the independent sector was politically
unacceptable?
– Yes, if you like. That you weren't taking on the real
issues. That, in a sense, you weren't in the real world.
– Ah, The Real World!

7
The Unum Necessarium

The power of maintaining discipline is the unum necessarium
*for a teacher; if he has not got it and cannot acquire it, he had
better sweep a crossing. It insults the soul, it is destructive of
all self-respect and dignity to be incessantly at the mercy of
boys. They are merciless, and the pathos of the situation never
touches them at all.*

A. C. BENSON (1902)

I do love that last sentence. It makes me smile and nod in
rueful recognition. The man who shaped that sentence not
only knew how to write, he knew the world of everyday teaching. He had lived and breathed in the classroom.

So: here is rule one, a rule often brutally spelt out by hard-
nosed teachers, and a rule that is as applicable to parents as it
is to those in the teaching profession: 'If you can't hold them,
you're stuffed. And don't expect any of the kids to feel sorry
for you. Because they won't.'

My father, who was not a very good disciplinarian as a
teacher or as a father – because he lost his temper all too
easily – often told my brother and me about his English master
at school. This was in the Rhondda Valley, a mining community with a fierce and justified pride in its grammar school
education. My father told this story so often that my brother
and I would sometimes silently join him in unison, mouthing
along with him, word for word.

No disrespect, because I'm the same now with my children
and with my pupils: it must be in the genes. Only the other
day in class I realised halfway through an anecdote that I had
told it to the same bunch not long before; something in their

eyes and in the general atmosphere suggested I had lost them. With less confidence and much worse timing I ploughed on with the story and afterwards raised my hand in apology, as a footballer does after a poor tackle or committing a foul, in a sad attempt to placate the referee and so avoid a booking.

'But,' I said, 'I hope you thought it was funny.'

'The first time,' someone called out. A condign punishment. And thank you.

Anyway, in the 1920s my father's English teacher, a Mr Jenkins, would stride into class, stand at his desk on the dais and face his unsettled mob.

'Boys,' Mr Jenkins looked at them all, 'I am waiting.' He stood stock still, hands on hips. His eyes roved the class.

'Boys,' eyeballs bulging, the veins on his neck fattening, 'I am still waiting.'

Unabated bedlam. Then Mr Jenkins' voice hit his favourite level.

'Boys, I shall not continue to wait!'

Here he slowly took off his jacket, rolled his sleeves up neatly to the elbow (as cricketers used to do), took off his belt and stormed up and down the rows of desks, laying about him on all sides.

'He spat lumps,' Dad would add, his eyes watering tears of admiration, as if Mr Jenkins was a man to emulate, a role model, a hero-villain in an early black and white Western.

Mr Jenkins, clearly, was a disastrous disciplinarian, and today he would have no strap to fall back on. Now he could not resort to the cane, to the ruler or to the slipper, all of which I was given as a child. I'm glad they're all gone. So, too, have most other sanctions. So, too, has any expression of normal human touch. Now you cannot put your arm round a pupil or lay a finger on anyone, even to praise the praiseworthy or to cheer the dejected. Our pupils have to be protected from teachers as if we're all potential paedophiles. If you want to talk to a pupil alone, leave your classroom door open. That's the professional advice. I ignore it.

There's no running away, however, from having to keep order yourself – in whatever way that can be achieved – and there never will be. Every now and then I worry that I might be losing it, and that anxiety visits you more as the years pass. Your pupils always stay the same age; you age; the gap widens. You fear you are out of touch. I have seen it happen to friends and colleagues of all ages. You notice they're looking shot to pieces. 'They just won't shut up,' they whisper at lunch or over a drink. Some teachers never have control, and I can't imagine a more gruelling way of spending a day. Some good teachers have it and lose it.

Throughout my career I have never taken for granted my discipline. You can be well prepared, you can be marking late at night, winning accolades for worthiness, up bright and early in the morning, be in your room before them, have a back-up plan and lots of visual aids, know their backgrounds and have covered every eventuality – but, if the sand starts to shift, if they won't shut up when you say, 'OK,' it is no place to be.

Discipline is a very different matter in different professions and in other organisations – even in those rightly famous for their rigour . . . I do remember a very distinguished fifty-year-old RAF officer who was training to be a teacher. For his teaching practice, he joined my school – hardly the toughest place to win your classroom spurs, but not without its challenges. At the end of his first week a kindly colleague asked him at lunch if he was having any difficulty with any of his classes. He bristled a little. 'Good God, no,' he said firmly. 'In my time I've put down a mutiny.' A fortnight later he was asking us about various pupils, wondering if they were as big a pest in our lessons as in his. Two weeks later, sadly, he was a nervous wreck.

Many a parent knows how difficult it can be to face an

unruly party of children in his own home. But how does it feel
to be a teacher facing a class? How apprehensive are you as
they walk in? Friends have often asked me to put my finger on
my state of mind. Any butterflies? It's not easy to generalise,
but I'll have a go at an ordinary day in my classroom.

It's an ordinary lesson, though there's no such thing, of
course, and I'm there in my room before they arrive. They
(you, if you prefer) come in. I stand by the door, watching
them come past me. I make as much eye-contact as I can, I
nod at a few, say 'hullo' here and there, a non-physical human
touch, how did you get on yesterday, or maybe tell a couple to
calm down. If the whole lot storm past you, throwing bags,
eyes wild and looking for action, you only have to check in
the timetable to see who taught them last and you'll know
there's another colleague with discipline problems.

I walk to my desk.

Right.

'OK, settle down.'

I could repeat that.

Come on, settle down now, and as I say it again I could look
you all in the eye, running my eye over each and every one of
you, to reinforce what I have said with a cold, coercive glare.

Or, I could, more selectively, Give An Evil to the potentially difficult ones among you, the proven difficult ones,
because I know who you are, believe me: I know you.

Or, choosing the non-confrontational route, I could avoid
any individual eye-contact, allowing my sight line to settle
just above your heads, as an actor does with his audience.
This would be friendly. I could then glance down at my notes,
giving you a little latitude, and so allow each and every one of
you a chance to settle down in your own time. That would be
nice, wouldn't it? That would be the more civilised, warm
move, and I do want to be friendly – after all, who wants to be
taught by a bastard? Besides, it's a pity to get off on the wrong

foot, so I'll do the decent thing and work on the basis that you are decent people and we all believe in reason and under-standing, in co-operation not competition. This would mean I am backing the liberal notion that, deep down, you know what is good for you and that in a while you will come to heel.

As you are doing.

Yes, I'll look at my lesson notes. I don't want a row, not first thing anyway, and after last night I feel like a quiet start. But what happens if, when I look up from reading my lesson notes (assuming I have written some, and if I haven't I'll just have to pretend I have), what happens if there isn't any sign at all of a quiet start, no semblance of a settling, in fact there's every bit as much inattention as there was when I first spoke, and now it's not only inattention, it's all building up to the point where, if I am to start teaching at all, I'll have to do something decisive. Something Dominating. Assert Control.

What happens if they rush me? Don't even think about it.

What would be my next move?

Well, never raise your voice. That's the usual advice to parents and to teachers. If you raise your voice, you're lost. That's what I was told, and you can see why. It's a good rule. Only the other day I was in the supermarket and two mothers, one in the cereal area and one next to the lamb chops, were scream-ing at their children. The one leaning over the lamb chops could be heard all over the shop. 'You do that again,' she said, 'and I'll kick you in the shins.' Well, she said 'f——— shins' in fact, but effing or not the children didn't take any notice. Not a blind bit. While it is distressing and sometimes fright-ening to see people lose their tempers, far more often it is sadly comic or simply embarrassing.

Mind you, there is also something demeaning about sound-ing querulous or plaintive, let alone appealing to their better natures. 'They are merciless,' as A. C. Benson rightly says, 'and the pathos of the situation never touches them at all.'

Besides, most days I can hear other teachers being querulous and other teachers shouting in their classrooms – as usual there's a terrific row coming at this moment from the biology department, and as usual it isn't working. Imagine shouting your way through a day. Imagine spending all day wrestling with a mob.

Or . . . I could use a very soft voice on you, which I've noticed many successful control freaks do. The power of the soft voice is based on the unspoken fear that if the softly spoken one ever does decide to act forcefully he will have the impact of a selective missile strike. The downside of the soft voice, though, is that it can sound as if the teacher feels he is in the company of a set of psychopaths and suspects that one false move could trigger them all off; or worse, it suggests an unctuously stroking approach, a desperate desire to ingratiate based on years of unreciprocated caring and deep disappointment. Anyway, pupils can always pretend they haven't heard a soft voice. What does the teacher do when shouting has failed and subtly soft assertion has not been spotted?

Far better for the teacher to believe in himself. Look up. Don't betray anxiety, don't be too chummy, don't patronise, don't talk to them as if they're children. Lots of negatives, I know, but they all add up to a positive. Believe you've got something of interest, something special, to tell them. Be yourself. Trust in your personality. Transfer your energy.

Getting a grip on a class may often be more a matter of getting a grip on one person. When I told my mother that I wanted to be a teacher too, she looked out of the window and said, 'There's always one, you know.' This idiomatic phrase took me somewhat aback. 'There's always one' to me meant 'There's always someone silly enough, or daft enough, there's always a fool in the world', and for a moment I thought she was saying I must be that one, a perversely foolish missionary, to follow my parents and to join so underpaid and beleaguered a profession.

In fact she was giving me her first tip on discipline. In every class, she suggested, there's always one you have to get on your side. There may be more than one, there may be a group, but even if there's a group or a mob or a clique, there's always a leader in there, and not necessarily the obvious one either, but the one the others look up to or at least look at or take their tone from. If you get that one on your side, she said, you'll be far less likely to have a problem.

Particularly in the first years of my teaching I found that invaluable advice, and in my last years I still do. I could name (but I won't) the current ones in all my classes. I asked my mother what to do once you had identified that boy or girl. What do I do next?

Don't look at him. Don't look for trouble. Imagine there is none. Keep your dignity. Move around. Get behind whoever it is, watch him only when he can't watch you. Stand just behind him as you teach, close but not too close, just out of sight, at a slightly unnerving distance. Talk softly into the back of his head, so that if he wants to talk to you or take you on he's lost his controlling field of vision.

Then move away just far enough and just long enough for him to relax and possibly even to smile at his accomplices; and then move back. Exactly the same place, only a little closer. He could then turn round and say something cheeky but I've found they rarely do. The point is: I haven't taken him on in front of the class, I haven't humiliated him in front of his cronies, and I haven't lost a public battle myself. A classroom battle can turn into a term-long war and can, in extreme cases, turn nasty – to obscene phone calls and even slashed tyres.

In most cases that stalking strategy is enough. Sometimes I'll also ask him a very easy question, one I know he can answer, and he'll gulp and get it right. He's glad he's got it right, it helps him with his cronies, and that might help me too. He might join my side. All this I learnt from my mother. She herself taught mostly in primary schools but also in secondary schools, and she definitely had The Look.

What is The Look? Without doubt some teachers have it. Some sportsmen have it. They walk into the classroom or on to the field of play and they look around. Batsman or teacher, it has nothing to do with height. Some of the smallest teachers and sportsmen have it. They look as if they belong. They look as if they are there by right. That's The Look. When I am ready I will begin. That is their body language. I am made for this stage. This is my chosen ground. I know I can perform.

Last week I was invited to attend a one-day workshop for teachers on Pupils Behaving Badly, a day in which I would learn how to handle aggressive students, parents and intruders. Two of the bullet points in defusing explosive behaviour were

- move position from enemy to ally
- use the energy from aggression to turn the tide

My mother would have contributed well to such workshops. I am not, of course, claiming that you can sort out all aggressive or difficult pupils. Try suggesting that to teachers who work in tough city areas or to teachers who have been assaulted. You cannot sort everyone out, and no one should listen to brassily overconfident teachers who claim never to have had any problems.

In my case, some of the most intellectually brilliant pupils I have taught, using words only, have pushed me to the limit, working to undermine the mutual respect I try so hard to establish. They're the mind-game psychos, the cynics with machetes. They're some of the ones I've had to face.

Talking of psychos, at the very beginning of his book

Psychotherapy, Anthony Storr – a doctor and psychiatrist – stresses the importance of the room in which the psychotherapist meets his patient, its lay-out, its atmosphere and decoration. As a teacher I would make the same claim. Your classroom, the place where you work, where you hope to inspire, is a crucial element in a teacher's professional performance, a potential help in his discipline and a key setting – to use a medical term – for successful practice. Generalising about classrooms is, I know, likely to invite ridicule from teachers who do not even have a room they can call their own, or teachers whose rooms are in so poor a state of repair that they will feel patronised or offended by anything I say. Even so, you have to make the very best of your place.

For some years I was peripatetic. I rushed along corridors, carrying piles of plays and exercise books, and found myself pushing open with my knee or foot the door of some awful maths room with bare grey walls, yellow ceiling and a blackboard full of equations, or a classics room with a lone late-nineteenth-century map of Ancient Greece in the fourth century BC, or the corner of an empty examination hall where the acoustics were so bad I developed a permanent sore throat. A teacher needs his space, his home.

Once I had my own room – I was nearly thirty – I spent many hours transforming it. Posters do furnish a room. So do cuttings from papers, postcards, wall hangings, photographs you have taken of places you love, poems and random bits of philosophy which make me smile or strike a subversive chord. Indeed I shall be weaving some of the poems from my classroom walls into this book. If my pupils become bored and allow their eyes to wander I want them to see something good.

I also have Bob Dylan, Bruce Springsteen and Van Morrison up there, the three greats of the last forty years (oh, come on, let's at least agree on the obvious truths), plus personal heroes like Arthur Miller, Miles Davis, Ben Webster,

Wordsworth and Edward Thomas. I have Philip Larkin look-ing wonderfully grumpy, and John Betjeman looking simply barking on the Cornish cliffs at Trebetherick, a place where my family have spent so many happy hours. Slotted around in any gaps left are Poems On The Underground and various talismans which, though tattered and much trimmed, I can't bear to part with: they're my friends. I love my classroom. I could go to sleep in it. Some of my pupils do.

From the day I started teaching I wanted to be a top teacher, and I wanted to stay teaching. Being a headmaster would have meant saying goodbye to the classroom. And in the classroom I have stayed. So, it follows that my room is bound, in an unspoken way, to tell my pupils about me. Your clothes, your walls, reveal you. Your pupils may or may not refer to your shirt or your tie or what's new on the walls but they do notice everything and they are more likely to respect the subject and you if they respect the room. They see where you're coming from, and having seen that, they are more likely to be interested, open and educable.

One of the liveliest teachers I've worked with not only had colourful walls but extended his welcome by playing a signa-ture tune, a different one for each class, as they walked in. They walked in to it and they walked in tall, with smiles of recognition (in both senses), lifted by the music, the team spirit and by the buoyancy of a teacher full of hope. For me that would not feel natural; it would feel over the top, and I wouldn't go that far, but for that teacher it was right. As a technique it may sound unpleasantly like *Dead Poets Society* but this move exactly caught and expressed that teacher's affection for his pupils and his respect for their world.

As many primary school teachers still do, my mother used to put up on the walls her pupils' art work, a big, bold display. With secondary-age pupils I have never done this. With poetry and creative prose my pupils write more freely, more personally, if they can trust you to keep it private. Puberty does that. It drives you inside. Writing often becomes a private line, a confessional, a revelation in a plain envelope which they usually prefer to remain that way. If they want to publish their work in school magazines or newspapers, fine. I encourage any who do.

From pride, from reflected glory, and in a celebratory spirit, I also pin up in my classroom photos of ex-pupils, literary pin-ups, those who have become or are becoming famous in the world of the arts: Vikram Seth, the novelist and poet, Christopher Reid, the poet and publisher, Vikram Jayanti, the film producer, Kit Hesketh-Harvey of 'Kit and the Widow', as well as younger ones who are beginning their journey. Their success gives me a thrill, a frisson that I may on one day or in one way, without even knowing it, have helped. Sometimes I catch their eye when I am teaching and I can see them again, exactly where they sat, hear their voices again and see their handwriting, even remember the colour of the ink they used. Kit Hesketh-Harvey was a brilliant reader of comic prose: I cried with laughter when he read from Evelyn Waugh's *Decline and Fall*. Christopher Reid, a delightfully warm and individual talent, drew witty cartoons. Vikram Seth, already an elegant stylist at seventeen, wrote in a large, clear, neat hand. Anthony Seldon, now a headmaster and political historian, wrote – in jet-black ink – in a neat, tiny hand, while Vikram Jayanti, bound for Hollywood, always preferred turquoise.

While I am not particularly interested in the exact lay-out of desks and tables, the one essential – especially for discipline – is to be able to see everyone's eyes. The small size of my room makes many configurations of desks and tables impossible, but even if I had a larger room I would still go for a conventional arrangement of rows or semi-circles. In this I may now be in a minority. Many colleagues, I notice, have their pupils sitting in groups of four, as if for a whist drive or bridge evening, all looking at each other, or working in pairs, or – I'm told – sharing, consulting and negotiating. Maybe they all are. I have to say, though, that when I pop into their rooms it seems they are consulting on the poems when the teacher is quite near them and consulting about Arsenal v. Tottenham when he is over there. What to some teachers is the happy buzz of team work to me feels too out of control, a cheerful anarchy. Still, they seem to like it. Nobody gets killed.

More interesting to me than the lay-out of the room is the fact that the difficult ones in my classes, the ones who make destructive comments, the intractable ones, the cleverly ineducable, the go-on-try-and-teach-me ones, always sit in the same place. It may be just me; it may be just my classroom. But it is spooky. *They sit in the same place.* There might as well be a plaque on the seat or a red light flashing over it, 'Shits and subversives sit here.' OK, so it's self-selecting and at least I know where they are, but my classroom, part of a converted flat, is so short of space that I really can't take my mother's advice and get round behind them without risking an accusation of homosexual assault or at the very least a whispered call to Childline.

Without a doubt humour, that saviour of many a marriage, is an essential in a teacher, and often vital for discipline. To feel its importance, you only have to think of all the humourless teachers and their boring lessons. A class full of laughter is a lovely feeling and sometimes it should be at the teacher's expense. Irony, accompanied by a quick smile, is the disciplinary form most often used by good teachers. It can be wonderfully effective, though it is galling to deliver a nicely timed ironic flick only to notice the intended victim is still talking to someone or is unaware the hit has landed.

Going down-market from irony, teachers are often told how terrible it is to be sarcastic. Certainly pupils resent it.

Certainly it should only be used as a last resort, when things are getting serious. But when I know the chips are down and it's them or me, or him or me, I'll go for the throat, no holds barred. It's not a pretty sight, I know, and it's a long way from the high moral ground, but there does come a point, like it or not, where it is a kind of shoot-out, a trial of strength, and blood has to be spilt and no prisoners taken. I look back on those incidents with no pleasure, but the alternative was a loss of control.

On a good day, on most days thank goodness, it does not come to this. But for some teachers the problem of keeping order, by whatever means, is always just around the corner or waiting in the next class. The teacher wakes up, feeling sick in the pit of his stomach, knowing that at 10.30 or at 2 o'clock in the afternoon, it will all happen again. The day is full of dread. You can help such a teacher, if he'll allow you, by looking at the lesson he's planning to see if it is on the most appropriate lines, though the lesson planned is rarely the problem. You can be in his room when his worst class arrives, playing the solidarity card. You can stay around for a little while, not too long, but long enough for the incoming pupils to see that you two are friends, that you like and support each other. Outside the classroom you can let the influential pupils in that class know how much you value that teacher and run stories to his advantage. But all this only takes the troubled teacher so far. Close the door for the last lesson on Friday afternoon, when the fruit flies, and you're on your own.

This is as true in the year 2000 as it was in A. C. Benson's privileged Eton of 1900. I began the chapter with a quotation from Benson and I'll end with his picture of a teacher who cannot control a class, even when his pupils wish that he could:

> Some of the boys resolved among themselves to try and
> stop this; they waited outside the room and implored

everyone to behave themselves; but it was impossible to
resist the impulse, and five minutes after the lesson had
begun the boy who had been the most urgent in his
entreaties was busily employed in constructing a long
rope of quill pens, which he pushed, as a sweeper pushes
his jointed brush, across the room to his friends opposite.

A boy was sent to see his tutor with a complaint of
serious insubordination. Little by little the story came
out, and it appeared that he had put a dormouse down
the master's back, between his neck and his collar, as he
sat correcting an exercise. 'How was I to know he drew
the line at a dormouse?' said the boy tearfully, giving a
dreadful glimpse of what had been tolerated.

Time for a poem from my classroom wall. The American
Robert Frost is one of my favourite writers. Not only that, but
during his stay in England (1911–14) he also persuaded his
friend Edward Thomas, one of my heroes, to 'drag himself out
from under the heap of his prose' and to turn to poetry. Just in
time, Edward Thomas took Robert Frost's advice, to catch a
language and an intonation 'fresh from talk', and found the
right road: out of their friendship a remarkable poet was born.

The poetry of Frost and Thomas is poetry not because it is
clever or exotic or shocking but, as Robert Nye puts it,
because it is better than anything prose can do. So, first a
poem by Robert Frost; then, a little later, a poem by Edward
Thomas.

8
The Road Not Taken

Two roads diverged in a yellow wood,
And sorry I could not travel both
And be one traveller, long I stood
And looked down one as far as I could
To where it bent in the undergrowth;

Then took the other, as just as fair,
And having perhaps the better claim,
Because it was grassy and wanted wear;
Though as for that the passing there
Had worn them really about the same,

And both that morning equally lay
In leaves no step had trodden black.
Oh, I kept the first for another day!
Yet knowing how way leads on to way,
I doubted if I ever should come back.

I shall be telling this with a sigh
Somewhere ages and ages hence:
Two roads diverged in a wood, and I –
I took the one less travelled by,
And that has made all the difference.

ROBERT FROST (1874–1963)

9
There's Always One

On the very first page of *Fortunata and Jacinta* (1887), the greatest Spanish novel of the late nineteenth century, Galdós describes two students sitting at the back of a lecture hall frying an egg while the professor meanders on about metaphysics. How very droll, a teacher might think, and how very Spanish, while comforting himself that the episode is only fiction. But a dormouse down the back of the Eton master's collar? That was a fact, wasn't it, and at much the same time. So, what about the mid-twentieth century in mid-Wales? Let me tell you some of the things we did to our teachers there in the 1950s.

As someone who has taken the teacher's road I find it hard to believe what I am about to describe. Indeed you may think I am making up these stories as much as Galdós did, or at the very least improving them. You may decide I am following the aesthetic imperative rather than the call of truth. I'm not.

Of course I cannot prove that I am telling it like it was. Our memories certainly play tricks on us and most autobiographies strike me as dangerous source material, if not more happily at home in the fiction genre. The following, however, did happen. I was in the room. Promise. What fascinates me now, though, is not so much the pupils' conduct as the teacher/victim's. Did he know? Could he have known? How could he not have known? How could he have known and gone on teaching? I now try to see myself sitting at his table at the front of the class as well as trying to see myself back at the desk where I used to sit. I'm not, by the way, going to bore you with our everyday pursuits, like all the boys in the front row staring fixedly at the master's flies until he went out to check his buttons. That was routine stuff.

But what about this?

In one classroom, high above the table where the teacher sat, there was a reinforcing rod, one of those iron bars which keep the roof from falling down and the walls from falling in. The bar was about eight feet above the teacher's seat and a few feet below the ceiling. A boy in my class, an expert fisherman – we were lucky enough to have the River Usk only yards away – tied a tiny lead weight to the end of a piece of cotton, and before the teacher came in the boy, with an expert cast, threw the lead weight over the iron bar.

Once the teacher had taken his seat, the boy, sitting on the far right of the front row, slowly let out the cotton reel. He had a pencil jammed inside the central hole of the reel so that, with a fisherman's practised skill, he could give out the cotton very carefully inch by inch. Don't ask me why the teacher did not see the cotton. He didn't.

The lead weight, about the size of a pea, slipped and swung down, like a spinning spider, until it was hanging a foot or so above the teacher's head. Then six inches above. We sat in appalled fascination. From the teacher's point of view we must have looked as if we were in a religious trance, heads tilted up slightly to the light, cataleptic, mouths open, eyes glazed, waiting for a call from God. There was no question of anyone laughing. This wasn't farce. This was way beyond the laughing league. This was high-risk stuff, dreadful, mystic, wonderful.

And the teacher had a temper. He was quite capable of going berserk. The danger was sensational. However cool the boy was, and he was cool, however quick-fingered he was, if the teacher suddenly stood up there was no way the boy could raise the spider in time. Slowly up and slowly down, there was no other possibility. Well, I suppose he could in panic have yanked it up but only at the risk of breaking the cotton and seeing the lead drop on the teacher's scalp.

This went on the whole lesson, the lead hovering. Then at last the lead went up. We breathed a collective sigh, thank God he's got away with it. Then the maniac returned for another bombing run, another Dambusters' raid, you could almost hear the Eric Coates sound track, letting the lead swing down again – no, no, please, enough's enough, we've got away with more than enough already – to see if he could lower it even closer, to see if he could brush the man's parting and make him scratch his head. The master did scratch his head but just missed the lead weight.

I can still feel the tension as I write this.

With another victim we played classroom cricket. This was not so much the work of a lone fisherman hero, this was one-in-all-in. On one side of the room sat the batting team; on the other side, the bowling. We tossed up before the lesson to decide which side was which. There were elaborate ground-rules, insisted upon by our scorer-umpire, a saintly scholar. The general thrust of the lesson-long contest was that the batting side scored runs by making the teacher come up with various stereotypical remarks of his. You scored one run for 'Oh, come on!', two for 'Good grief, I've just told you that!', three runs for 'Pull yourself together, boy!', four for 'What on earth have you been doing all this term!' and six for 'One more squeak out of you and it's detention!'

The batting side spent the whole forty minutes not learn-ing French but asking any kind of damn-fool questions to ensure the teacher said any of the run-scoring phrases. As the total grew the batters occasionally clapped, calling out, 'Shot!' The aim of the bowling side was more limited. It was to make the teacher say only one phrase, 'You silly boy!' Every time he said 'You silly boy!' you bowled out a batsman, you took a wicket. But to make him say 'You silly boy!' ten times in forty minutes, i.e. to bowl a side out, was extremely difficult. Clearly conditions favoured batting. With a greater range of options the batters became more and more smug, grinning, nodding, and giving each other the thumbs-up as they knocked the ball around, picking up a 'Good grief!' here and a 'Pull yourself together!' there, while the bowlers, ever more desperate for a breakthrough, sprayed it all over the place.

With seven wickets down and less than a minute to go, the umpire-scorer whispered, 'Last over.' One kamikaze bowler now risked his all on a question so brain-dead, so mindless, so asking-for-it that he risked being hit for six, three hours' detention, but the teacher cracked, banged his fists on his table in fury and shouted:

'You silly, silly, SILLY boy!'

At which the bowler screamed:

'Hat-trick!'

(I failed O-level French.)

But what about how I have been treated as a teacher? Ever any sense that a plot was afoot? Anything silly, nasty . . . lead weights, knife attacks? Of course I probably wouldn't know them all. I could well have not picked up their games, and they're not exactly going to come up afterwards and tell me what they've got away with, are they?

When I said earlier that the worst Ones I have dealt with always sit in the same place it wasn't strictly true. The absolutely worst pupil I've ever taught, though taught isn't the word, sat smack bang in the middle row, as central and as in my line of vision as it was possible to be.

In December 1973 I set off with my wife and baby daughter for Australia. That was the time of the three-day week, with strikes on everywhere. 'Who rules the country,' Mr Heath asked the nation, 'an elected government or the unions?' 'Not sure,' a colleague wrote in my pigeonhole, 'but a rat leaves the sinking ship,' pinning this to a caricature of me swimming for the Antipodes while the good ship SS *Great Britain* sank beneath the waves. That year in Melbourne, a year of talking to babies in prams, the first of three important educational visits to Australia, was a crucial one for me as a teacher. I learnt so much from my time in the classroom and so much from other teachers.

In 1974 I was thirty-two. I had been teaching for ten years, and after ten years I knew I could teach. Without being over-confident (if anything I have never been sufficiently confident) I had already taught at all levels and at all the secondary school ages, produced plays, run teams, faced disciplinary challenges, sat on committees, learnt which buttons to press, which colleagues to trust, and finessed a few of the political angles. Nor were the 1960s and 1970s the easiest of years to be a teacher. I won't run through the cliché snapshots of that overdiscussed time but respect for authority in general and for teachers in particular was certainly hard earned. So I felt I had served my apprenticeship, not in an inner-city school, true, but a worthwhile apprenticeship all the same.

In my fourth form class of that year there were twenty-nine pupils. But, as far as I was concerned, there was only One. This One could destroy any helpful atmosphere I'd created by methods and strategies so subtle, so devious, so hard to read, so seeming-innocent that it amounted to an evil genius: Iago springs to mind. Like Iago he enjoyed bonhomie; like

Iago he was the joker in the pack, a matey chameleon. He chose the exact moment to make his move, and he moved by instinct, surfing the precise second when the lesson was going well, e.g. a poem being sensitively read by a shy pupil or a scene of a play coming alive with everyone absorbed in its world, or someone (previously vulnerable but taciturn) beginning to talk more freely about his thoughts and feelings. In a word: moments when I was winning. These were the moments he struck, during the experiences every teacher treasures, when it is a job that gives rewards beyond price, when the teacher feels (as D. H. Lawrence fulsomely but all too briefly did) that the job is the noblest profession:

> As tendrils reach out yearningly,
> Slowly rotate until they reach the tree
> That they cleave unto, and up which they climb
> Up to their lives – so they to me.
>
> I feel them cling and cleave to me
> As vines going eagerly up; they twine
> My life with other leaves, my time
> Is hidden in theirs, their thrills are mine.

At such a moment of greatest sharing, of public intimacy if you like, of education at its best, he would lightly drum his feet, but so lightly, in so underplayed a way, that you could barely call it drumming. You heard it, the class heard it, he knew you heard it, and if you said, 'Who's doing that?' he would ease off so easily, like a drummer, like Tony Williams playing with Miles Davis, fading his brushes into a percussive texture of nothingness, and all done so smoothly on the fade that if he replied, 'Doing what?' to your question, everyone else, though they had heard it too, would echo, 'Yes, what?'

Or he would make a contribution so close to sincerity yet so akin to mockery that it wore the same face. In a second he could alter the focus so that I was no longer teaching the whole class, and I believe in whole class teaching, but playing verbal squash or tennis only with him, though it felt more like a shoot-out. The unspoken agenda was:

'You know I'm wrecking your lesson, Smith, you Pommie prat, and you're powerless.'

'And I know what you're up to, you little bastard, but I can't fix you.'

Whatever my mood or personal ups and downs, whatever the stresses at home, I've always tried to remain self-controlled and balanced in class, to stay open and tolerant. That control, even in the face of criticism that I am too controlled and possibly too controlling, has been the main professional model I have set myself: to have fun, but to listen to others with respect, however taxing that is. Though it is difficult to live up to, that is the feel I am after. My 'One' instinctively knew that; he played on it, he played on it hard. When they tried to play on him, Hamlet sorted out Rosencrantz and Guildenstern in no time. I would like to have seen Hamlet sort this bloke out.

So I would build in his double-edged offering, choosing to ignore the destructive side. I would include his comment, channelling his aggression as if it were a contribution. To an extent that worked because I was refusing to fight. So he switched tactics. As one boy was talking about his grandmother, the One wove a small flower into his own hair, sweetly smiling. That finished off that boy. In the school yard, after lunch on a scorching day, I saw him knock another boy's glasses off and tread on them. I was so incoherent with anger that I rushed out but only strangled sounds came out of my mouth. In a very reasonable voice he explained that it was an accident.

He was good-looking and fresh-faced, the nicest school

portrait any mother could wish to see on her piano or man-
telpiece. On an identity parade you would not have picked
him out. I had never really believed in *Lord of the Flies*, and it
is still not a book that I greatly admire, but one boy in 1974
made me rethink my position.

'Are you going to treat a man as what he is, or as what he
might be?' William Temple asks us. 'Morality requires, I think,
that you should treat him as what he might be, as what he has
it in him to become.' The idealism of Temple's words has
inspired me and many other teachers, but in the case of this
boy I simply could not measure up. Occasionally I looked into
his eyes, not giving him An Evil, but trying to see deeper into
him. I saw nothing. The closest I came to encountering the
same response was when I was on holiday with my family in
Sydney. Going round an aquarium I looked, through the safety
of a very thick pane of glass, into the eyes of a tiger shark. The
shark returned a blank, pitiless stare.

My God, I thought, it's him.

After a term of this, my head of department – a man I infi-
nitely admired – offered to swap classes with me. He knew I
was struggling. I'd made no bones about that. I could, he said,
take his lot and he'd take mine; then I could enjoy the rest of
my year in Australia. We even had a laugh about it; he suggested, for my last lesson with them, that I took into class
D. H. Lawrence's 'Last Lesson of the Afternoon':

When will the bell ring, and end this weariness?
How long have they tugged the leash, and strained apart
My pack of unruly hounds! I cannot start
Them again on a quarry of knowledge they hate to hunt,
I can haul them and urge them no more.

No longer now can I endure the brunt
Of all the books that lie out on the desks; a full threescore

Of several insults of blotted pages, and scrawl
Of slovenly work that they have offered me?
I am sick, and what on earth is the good of it all?
What good to them or me, I cannot see!

So, shall I take
My last dear fuel of life to heap on my soul
And kindle my will to a flame that shall consume
Their dross of indifference; and take the toll
Of their insults in punishment? — I will not! —

I will not waste my soul and my strength for this.
What do I care for all that they do amiss!
What is the point of this teaching of mine, and of this
Learning of theirs? It all goes down the same abyss.

What does it matter to me, if they can write
A description of a dog, or if they can't?
What is the point? To us both, it is all my aunt!
And yet I'm supposed to care, with all my might.

I do not, and will not; they won't and they don't; and that's all!
I shall keep my strength for myself; they can keep theirs as well.
Why should we beat our heads against the wall
Of each other? I shall sit and wait for the bell.

But I wasn't D. H. Lawrence and they weren't a pack of unruly hounds: there was just one. I wasn't going to wait for the bell or for the end of the term or for the end of the year. D. H. Lawrence gave up teaching and I intended going on. My pride was hurt and challenged. It did matter to me. It mattered to me that they could write and it mattered to me that they listened. And it mattered very much to me that one boy could screw the whole thing up. Not only was I 'supposed to care' about what was going amiss, I did care. I did not want to lose. And I would not! 'I will not!'

So I turned down my head of department's kind offer, and I hope the other twenty-eight pupils enjoyed English for the rest of the year. Some colleagues said later that I had won but it never felt like that.

Apart from some obscene phone calls to my wife (I knew it was him, he was especially friendly on the mornings after) he eventually eased off. I have never worked out what caused all this. Was it something trivial, such as my English accent, which strikes some Australians as arrogant? Perhaps he disliked my style. Perhaps he just couldn't stand my guts: that's the simplest. Whatever it was, causing havoc gave him a warm feeling inside, and seeing my hands and mouth shake made his day. It was the only thing in that excellent year in Australia which made me feel sick deep in the pit of my stomach . . . 'Oh, no, I've got him again third lesson. Get me back to England! Not to D. H. Lawrence, but to a bit of Edward Thomas and "Adlestrop".'

10
Adlestrop

Yes, I remember Adlestrop –
The name, because one afternoon
Of heat the express-train drew up there
Unwontedly. It was late June.

The steam hissed. Someone cleared his throat.
No one left and no one came
On that bare platform. What I saw
Was Adlestrop – only the name

And willows, willow-herb, and grass,
And meadowsweet, and haycocks dry,
No whit less still and lonely fair
Than the high cloudlets in the sky.

And for that minute a blackbird sang
Close by, and round him, mistier,
Farther and farther, all the birds
Of Oxfordshire and Gloucestershire.

EDWARD THOMAS (1878–1917)

11
Winston Churchill Learns Latin

When the last sound of my mother's departing wheels had died away, the Headmaster invited me to hand over any money I had in my possession. I produced my three half-crowns, which were duly entered in a book, and I was told that from time to time there would be a 'shop' at the school with all sorts of things which one would like to have, and that I could choose what I liked up to the limit of the seven and sixpence. Then we quitted the Headmaster's parlour and the comfortable private side of the house, and entered the more bleak apartments reserved for the instruction and accommodation of the pupils. I was taken into a Form Room and told to sit at a desk. All the other boys were out of doors, and I was alone with the Form Master. He produced a thin greeny-brown-covered book filled with words in different types of print.

'You have never done any Latin before, have you?' he said.

'No, sir.'

'This is a Latin grammar.' He opened it at a well-thumbed page. 'You must learn this,' he said, pointing to a number of words in a frame of lines. 'I will come back in half an hour and see what you know.'

Behold me then on a gloomy evening, with an aching heart, seated in front of the First Declension.

Mensa	a table
Mensa	O table
Mensam	a table
Mensae	of a table
Mensae	to or for a table
Mensa	by, with or from a table

What on earth did it mean? Where was the sense in it? It seemed absolute rigmarole to me. However, there was one thing I could always do: I could learn by heart. And I thereupon proceeded, as far as my private sorrows would allow, to memorise the acrostic-looking task which had been set me.

In due course the Master returned.

'Have you learnt it?' he asked.

'I think I can *say* it, sir,' I replied; and I gabbled it off.

He seemed so satisfied with this that I was emboldened to ask a question.

'What does it mean, sir?'

'It means what it says. Mensa, a table. Mensa is a noun of the First Declension. There are five declensions. You have learnt the singular of the First Declension.'

'But,' I repeated, 'what does it mean?'

'Mensa means a table,' he answered.

'Then why does mensa also mean O table,' I enquired, 'and what does O table mean?'

'Mensa, O table, is the vocative case,' he replied.

'But why O table?' I persisted in genuine curiosity.

'O table – you would use that in addressing a table, in

invoking a table.' And then seeing he was not carrying me with him, 'You would use it in speaking to a table.'

'But I never do,' I blurted out in honest amazement.

'If you are impertinent, you will be punished, and punished, let me tell you, very severely,' was his conclusive rejoinder.

Such was my first introduction to the Classics from which, I have been told, many of our cleverest men have derived so much solace and profit.

from *My Early Life*

12
Role Models

As a seven-year-old child I woke up to the sound of a primary school playground. In 1949, my father, back from the war and back in the classroom, had been appointed the head teacher of a school in north Bristol, so we moved away from Uncle Bert and Grandad and the lanes of rural Gloucestershire to settle into The School House, Patchway. From a large home in a small village to a tiny place on the edge of a housing estate.

School – my school, my father and my mother's school – was now just the other side of my bedroom wall. School was everywhere, inside the house and outside. After a day of school my parents now added Night School. School was life. I no longer walked two miles of farming country to Berkeley, I walked the five yards to Patchway. I only had to cross the back yard to smell the air of the classrooms and to breathe in the chalk dust.

If that wasn't enough, at the weekends other head teachers and their families came to tea. Even in the summer holidays there was little respite because, if we went away to the seaside for a week, we would share a place with other state school teachers and the talk would always be teacher-talk: HMIs, the 11-plus, difficult families, Raising The School Leaving Age and so on.

All this should have been enough to put any child off the profession, but I still see my parents, in their very different ways, as model teachers. Teachers often base their practice, consciously or unconsciously, on the models they best remember from their own school and university days. Or on the models they most value. Teachers love to talk of their own teachers, of those who first inspired them with a love of their subject, and I am no exception, except that in my case it has to start with my family. After Uncle Bert's early influence it was my parents whose example led me to follow them, and I have never regretted it. When I went through a rather snobbish phase and insisted on saying I was a 'schoolmaster' not a 'teacher', my father said Jesus was a teacher and he wasn't ashamed of it, and that was good enough for him.

Our front door was knocked at all hours of the day and night, sometimes by tramps, because those mid-nineteenth-century Church of England school houses looked a little like a small vicarage and the clergy were seen as likely sources for charity. More often, though, it was simply parents asking us if we would mind opening up the school because 'Our Victor's left his satchel' or 'Our Carol's been and left her plimsolls' or 'Our Brian's left his coat. It's all right, Mr Smith, I've already hit him.' That's what it's like if you live over the shop.

In the holidays, or during non-school hours, my father would usually be in the school working. It was only five yards from our back door. (I've spent my life over the shop, too: I tend to do the same.) Quite often he was just tidying up, or escaping us, or more likely he was writing out lists in his beautiful manuscript lettering, either on to parchment or on to thick cartridge paper. Both the school and the local church walls were full of psalms and prayers set out on his illuminated parchments. With his pen in his hand there was no stopping him. He even wrote out the staff playground rotas and lavatory duty rotas as if they were the Book of Kells. I've often wondered if my later love of Eric Gill's lettering and engraving goes back to watching my father's broad nib form those letters. In his hands even a word as common as 'and' could look so grand and so powerful. In the right hands, it is.

Talking of lavatories, for some reason in that part of north Bristol we called them 'the offices'. Hands were always going up in my mother or father's class.

'Please, Miss, c'n I go to th'offices?'

'Miss, Brenda's bursting.'

'Miss, she's got to go!'

Across the playground there was a red-brick outbuilding, 'the offices' themselves, with tiny low seats, and if anything went wrong in the offices, anything worse than a boy misfiring, there was an enquiry. Dad, always very hot on personal hygiene, would demand to know who had made the mess. No one owned up. No one ever does. They sit it out. Never expect a class, let alone a larger group, to deliver you a shamefaced culprit, particularly in that field of human conduct. Just imagine the smelly poo-poo noises. Who'd run that gauntlet? No one in the classroom moved a muscle. Only eyes flickered and cheeks burned.

'So, no one made the mess?'

Not a hand in sight.

'No one?'

No.

'In which case you will all stay here until the girl or boy who *did* make that mess owns up.'

Big Mistake, Dad.

'Mr Smith, my mum's in hospital.'

'Miss, I got to go to cubs.'

'Miss, my dad's taking me roller-skating.'

Every teacher, male or female, could be called 'Miss'. Teacher was invariably a feminine noun.

'No one will go anywhere! You will all stay here. Someone knows who it is.'

Shufflings and glares and a lengthening silence. My mother would then whisper to my father:

'You're a fool. You'll be here all night.'

'If I have to be, I will be.'

'On your own head be it.'

'Right,' Dad said, on the edge of one of his rages, 'David Smith will go and clear it up!'

Or, as a variant:

'Right, Jonathan Smith will go and clear it up!'

In this way I learnt two things: as a teacher, never talk yourself into a disciplinary corner; and, as a pupil, accept the fact that life can be unfair. Especially if your dad's the head teacher.

I saw both my parents as teachers at close quarters, all day, every day, before, during and after school. I was one of their pupils. How many people have been taught at school by both their parents? I saw what they put into the job and, as I grew older, I discovered what it took out of them. Both were ill in their fifties, both illnesses stress-related. Each day, fifteen minutes after school ended, I watched them slump into their armchairs and fall straight asleep. I now know how they felt.

Both could captivate a class. My father did it with his Welsh wit and repartee, with buzz and bursts of energy, his nervous impulses and his determination to win a class clear in the tension on his face. I still try to emulate that style when I'm feeling 'up' for a lesson. Some days, often (strangely enough) when I am exhausted, I go in determined to turn it on and perform and, while performing, I run right to the very end of my capacity. I drain the well dry. I can feel my face go white. After teaching like that I feel so spent I am not really with the people who are talking to me. I can hear them but I don't grasp it. The only other time I feel that is when I am writing a book.

As for my writing when I was nine, I have before me my English exercise book for 1951. In it there are letters, compositions, prayers, dictations, proverbs, punctuation tests, spelling lists, helpful hints on linking sentences, the use of the apostrophe and, for handwriting practice, a short sentence containing all the letters of the alphabet: 'I packed my box with five dozen liquor jugs.' This grey exercise book is notable more for its neatness and accuracy than for its imaginative range. With most nine-year-olds now, fifty years later, my guess is that the reverse would be the case.

Every piece was toughly marked by my father, revealing the rather mean Smith streak as a marker which I inherited. For most of my career I held to that. Mind you, to keep in tune with current practice, the last few years I'm so into positive marking I'm throwing inflated grades at all and sundry. Mark rigorously now and they'll want to change sets, if not subjects, if not examination boards, so now absolutely everyone's doing wonderfully well in my classes. The least they get is an A: they won't settle for less. But why didn't I get A*? I demand a remark. If the remark goes against me I'm going all the way to the tribunal. Pass marks are up, everything's up. Give them all 90 per cent and you're a great teacher.

My father liked to keep his pupils on their toes. He felt your class should not come in always knowing what to expect or sure of what mood you would be in. I agree, though you do need a core steadiness; and the unpredictable buzz approach does demand very high adrenalin. If you teach like that you must find a strategy, an overall view of the day, that allows you to pace yourself. Pacing yourself is your safety net; every now and then you need to build into your morning or afternoon what I call a bread-and-butter lesson, a quiet tick-over when you recoup some energy. If I have five lessons in a row I try to make one less demanding. With his mercurial restless nature, my father may well have found it hard to establish a consistent game. He was all for snapping at their heels, always looking to challenge and provoke. When it did not work, he flared.

My mother had no such problems. Although she was able to improvise as she went along, her strength was that she was completely in control; the pupils felt safe with her and trusted her. She was The Boss. She had The Look. In her room you sensed unquestioning respect. From her I learnt the value of such respect, without which a teacher is doomed to be second rate or en route to becoming a nervous wreck.

Over the years I have tried to graft on the ability to deflect, to have fun, to adapt and to edit. If you stick slavishly to the script at any level, but particularly with the most able pupils, you will not bring out the best in them. That is why, however much importance you set by lesson preparation (and my parents were both well prepared), that is only a start. As a teacher you're not only a writer, but an actor, a parent, a director and an improviser – it's not so much a Hollywood epic as a low-budget movie with a hand-held camera.

Big Question. Well, a big question for me: what prompted my parents, professionally trained school teachers and members of the NUT, teachers who (day and night) lived and breathed the local community, to send me not to the local grammar school but to a small independent school in Wales? Yes, true, it was at least Wales, and my father was what the English would call very Welsh, but he had been brought up in the Rhondda and greatly valued his own grammar school education, and that was a very different tradition from the public schools. Also, as far as I can recall, we did not know a single public school person, apart from the vicar, and the vicar often told us how unhappy he had been at his boarding school.

True, too, that my brother had not settled particularly well at the local grammar school, but then lots of pupils, especially a teacher's children, take a little while to settle. Perhaps my father wanted to re-establish a foothold in Wales – the Welsh, more than most, feel that tug, and one of his brothers lived near Brecon – though a fee-paying independent school founded in 1541 at the foot of the Brecon Beacons was hardly in tune with his background.

My father was the least snobbish, the least status-conscious man I have ever met, so he certainly wasn't interested in the family going up-market. Perhaps my parents sensed it had all been a bit too much for their children to be at school all day and then to be at school at home in the evening, with both of them hanging over our homework, telling us to rethink this, not to be stupid and to redo that. That is a terrible temptation for teacher-parents, and one I have lived with as a son and as a father.

Whatever the reason, as a ten-year-old I followed my brother to Christ College, Brecon, where he had already proved to be not only much happier but quick to make friends, friends who have remained very close to him through-out his life. For me, a young boy who had often been ill, the great advantage was that I toughened up. That is said without a shred of embarrassment or macho pride or criticism. It is a simple fact. I am not keen on the school of hard knocks phi-losophy, particularly in education, but it is true that while away from home I became physically and mentally more resilient. Having once been fussy and liable to hide bits of bacon (which I called shrapnel) in my trouser pocket, I now ate everything, I was rarely ill, I loved walking in the hills and I enjoyed the games.

When my own children were school age my wife and I did not want them to go away and board, and they didn't. Becky sometimes said she wanted to, no doubt to get well away from us, but that passed; it was an option that Edward never contemplated. But for me, without a doubt, the boarding experience had considerable value. Paradoxically I would have hated not having my own children at home as they grew up, even through the difficult teens, yet I readily accept what I may well have missed at that stage of my own development.

And what of my role models at Christ College, who were those 'special teachers'? Here I can start with a specific date. My outstanding memory of 1953, my second year as a boarder at Brecon, is not of the spacious playing fields or the Queen's Coronation or the Ashes victory or of Hillary and Tensing climbing Everest but of my English master, Bob Jones, being very upset when Kathleen Ferrier, the contralto, died so young.

My God, I thought, he's crying. He's in tears. He stood there in front of us, the tears rolling down his cheeks. Later that week I heard a record of Kathleen Ferrier singing 'Oh, for the wings, for the wings of a dove' and I knew why. I still feel it when I hear her singing 'What is life?' or 'Art thou troubled?' or 'Ombra mai fu'. Her passionate, unaffected voice stops me in my tracks and makes me think of that moment in October 1953 with a young teacher standing there so full of emotion. From then on I felt an unspoken bond developing with Bob Jones. He was quite a severe man in some ways, so the bond remained unspoken, but a teacher – especially a sharply critical one – being seen to have an emotional and intellectual life of his own made a big impression on me.

It seems a little disloyal to my parents to point out the weaknesses of an education which asked of them so much financial self-sacrifice and self-denial, but during my years away at school only Bob Jones and one other teacher stand out. That is partly because the curriculum and the ethos were remarkably similar to the curriculum and ethos criticised at

Eton in the 1890s by A. C. Benson: a criticism of the inviola-
bility of the classics.

While the pastoral side was excellent – my housemaster,
Rex Morgan, was a most caring priest – there was little intellectual excitement or tension in the school, which meant it
attracted few inspiring teachers. Things improved markedly
with a new head in 1956, but for most of my time the prep
rooms were full of Livy, Virgil and Xenophon. The most
thumbed books were classical dictionaries and primers,
Kennedy and North and Hillard. For the three or four boys in
the school who were excellent classicists this was fine.

I was taught no science; not one lesson. I was taught no art
or music. Modern languages were a disaster area. The assumption was that if you were able you did classics, and even if you
weren't able there was a strong chance that classics was what
you would end up doing. This is not an argument against the
study of classics, for which I have the deepest respect, but
against a self-satisfied educational élite without the imagina-
tion or the humility to see how inappropriate this curriculum
was. When I tell them all this, people shake their heads; they
remind me that this was after the Second World War, for
God's sake, this was the 1950s not the 1890s. I know. It sounds
mad and it was mad.

Bob Jones, like Kathleen Ferrier, died far too young, but he
taught literature with a religious rigour. Indeed he taught it as
if his life depended on it. English literature, not classics, was
the central discipline to him. His eyes burned. His classroom
felt more like chapel than chapel. He had been a pupil, which
means a disciple, of F. R. Leavis at Downing College,
Cambridge, and he brought some of that personal edge and
combative partisanship to his lessons. I didn't quite know
what was going on but something was and I liked the smell of
uncompromising contempt: always heady stuff for an unresolved boy. It meant you could put your boot in.

More importantly for my future as a teacher, I was taught history by an extraordinary man, a short, bald man called Doug Inglis. Doug had not been to Cambridge. He had a first-class degree from Liverpool, a fact he liked to drop and a fact he liked to stress, further stressing that no one else on the staff had a first-class degree, and muttering only a little more quietly that quite a few had degrees he'd better not mention from universities he'd rather not say. (How pupils love gossip. Almost as much as they hate political correctness.)

Outwardly, Doug did the same things every day in the same order and at the same metronomic pace. He walked in on time, opened his leather attaché case, and took out his neat notes all written in his large hand. He then wiped his glasses, wiped his mouth (his false teeth did not fit too well), folded his handkerchief, told us a scurrilous anecdote, told us what book he was reading last night, told us why it was interesting and added that he didn't give a damn if we were interested or not because he was. Then he picked up a piece of chalk, tapped it like a cigarette and zapped us with the real stuff. Serious History. In his manner and his method he distanced himself from teachers who wasted hours every day doing things they should have avoided. Like A. C. Benson he despised people who made a virtue out of drudgery.

I watched his every move. Here was a teacher, a model teacher of a kind, who played up to his caricature, knowing we were copying all his rituals, his every gesture, miming his opening his case, wiping his glasses, wiping his mouth and folding his handkerchief. We even mimicked his cackle. When he cackled at his own jokes we cackled too, not so much in open mockery as in a kind of team effort, a supporting chorus from the massed ranks on the terraces. For him that was an acceptable part of the game. What was unacceptable was not to do the reading he set. Fail to do the reading and he savaged you.

Again – and I cannot overstress this – he had an intellectual life of his own. I could see it in every lesson: he talked not only history, but politics, economics, journals, novels, newspapers, specialist magazines and libraries. He made me feel I could be an intellectual, indeed that I already was one – that glamorous game works – and that he judged me not from the moral but from the intellectual standpoint. And, when you're young, what a blessed relief that is.

His example prompted me to be proud of my favourite subjects (history and English), to feel that I had made absolutely the right choice in not going all the way with classics (I had studied Latin and Greek), and also encouraged my already half-formed distaste for a certain kind of public school self-satisfaction. He was somewhat ill at ease socially, as I felt I was and feel I still am, and he backed away from those who reeked of geniality. He was down to earth, with none of Benson's susceptibility to boyish charm or athletic bodies. He had little time for that part of the profession which appeals to those with tortured personalities, private codes and camp networks.

He loved golf but loathed the glorification of sport. On Monday mornings he would always ask me what I had been reading over the weekend, and then press me to tell him about it in a little more detail. That subsidiary question was a necessary corrective to a teenager toying with intellectual dishonesty. He never asked me how I got on in rugby or how many runs I made in cricket. In other words, our world was not his, a crucial distinction teachers should remember.

His main purpose was to capture your interest, to fascinate you into taking the subject seriously. If you took it seriously, it became fun. If you became absorbed, you loved it. That included the holidays. Brainless beach holidays were, he assured me, over-rated. He was right. I should read. Read, then I would have something in my head and the beginnings of an interior life. Most of the staff, he confided, never read a book in term-time (too busy) or in the holidays (somehow never got round to it). Cackle.

Doug Inglis's love of history still burns in me. Even more, he drew me into the world of good books and big ideas. By the time I left school (in 1960) for university I was well on my way to becoming a teacher – not that I would have dreamt of admitting it to my friends.

There are three main strands in the teaching at Cambridge: a weekly one-hour supervision (a don teaching one or two undergraduates), seminars (small discussion classes) and public lectures. Not surprisingly, the weekly supervision is the central, most intense experience. If it goes well it can prove a life-long influence.

By 1960, when I arrived at St John's, the controversial school of Cambridge English had passed its strident high noon. Though 'reading English' was still a tick in most boxes and in most circles, it did not feel a particularly exciting era to be there. The confidence that English was the central discipline had peaked, the exclusion of history and biography from literary studies was over, as indeed was much of the partisan passion.

True, there was the bitter Two Cultures clash between C. P. Snow and F. R. Leavis; there was the question mark over George Steiner (was he an international, multi-cultural scholar who exposed Cambridge parochialism, or something rather less than that?); and there was a last sight of C. S. Lewis. Coming in was the socialism of Raymond Williams, while the critics were already putting an historical frame around the place. I did not like the past-tense sound of 'Cambridge English, from I. A. Richards to F. R. Leavis'. Had I missed the action? Where were those heady days of high analytical fervour when you would kill over the moral

importance of George Eliot or cut someone dead over a culpably misread ambiguity?

Even so, whichever decade or century I arrived there, I had
before me the shining example of talent. Wordsworth ('a
stripling of the hills/A Northern villager') had been at St
John's, and no one, before or since, has described residence in
Cambridge and the feel of undergraduate life with more pin-
point accuracy and psychological penetration than
Wordsworth in Book Three of *The Prelude*.

Furthermore, as a future teacher, I was very keen to see
how I would be supervised. One thing was certain: I, a
stripling from Wales and the West, needed to be taught. I
wanted to be taught. I was educable (and I still am). But
would I be out of my depth? Or would the dons prove to be
like schoolteachers, just cleverer and even more unworldly,
but basically an extreme form of the same breed? Whichever,
I did not want to be a victim of the increasingly fashionable
FOFO school of teaching (fuck off and find out for yourself).

My weekly supervisions came with two very different schol-
ars and men: Hugh Sykes Davies, the novelist, poet and critic,
and George Watson, the literary historian, critic and bibliog-
rapher. Hugh was much married, George a bachelor.

Hugh Sykes Davies, a colourful and multi-talented figure,
had a life-long connection with St John's, from his undergraduate days to Director of Studies. He was a brilliant
story-teller, broadcaster and wit. He knew the classics and he
knew Italian. He knew women and he knew how to mix a
drink. His way of teaching was conversational, anecdotal,
charming and tangental.

I am not sure if he bothered to read my weekly essays (in
charitable moments I like to think that he did) but in three
years of supervisions he never put a mark of any kind on any
of them. I suspect they bored him, which (though perhaps
understandable) is not good enough. You have, as a teacher, to

mask your boredom. Without referring to my essay we would, however, discuss the author I was reading that week, often as if Hugh had just come in from having a drink or a country walk with one or all of them: Smollett, Dante, Sophocles, Donne, Shakespeare, Clare, Hopkins, Fielding, T. S. Eliot ('Tommy') and, of course, Wordsworth. He knew more about Wordsworth, particularly Wordsworth's language, than any scholar I have read or met. For that, not to mention everything else, I owe him an incalculable debt: Wordsworth was the prevailing creative presence in Hugh's life, as he has been in mine.

Sitting in his dark rooms in New Court, puffing the largest pipe I have ever seen and overlooking the spot where grew Wordsworth's famous ash tree ('that tree, Jonathan, was the only really intimate friend he made at Cambridge'), Hugh slid seamlessly back and forth from practical criticism to the Bible to personal reflections on rivers and fishing and women and guilt.

We discussed how Wordsworth used *The Prelude*, among other things, as a confessional: how the poet admitted, as one would to a priest, his minor sins, e.g., that in his boyhood days he had robbed birds' nests, stolen game from the traps of other hunters, and even taken someone else's boat out on the lake. But he did not write at all about his much greater offence: that, as a man, he left Annette Vallon, his pregnant girlfriend, behind in revolutionary France while he scurried back to England. Given that the most interesting revelations often don't find their way into diaries and confessionals, the later passage in which Wordsworth describes how he was suddenly arrested by the sight of a bare gibbet on an open plain now seemed a subtle revelation. After all his transgressions, and particularly over the major one he did not admit, Wordsworth probably thought – on a powerfully imaginative level – that he himself was lucky to have escaped the hangman. And who knows, he may have had even graver matters on his conscience.

That was the kind of personal-literary-psychological talk Hugh Sykes Davies and I had. Without telling him I had done so, I also read his poetry and five novels (what, I wondered, was *he* leaving out?) and he told me about his long dipsomaniac lunches with Malcolm Lowry, the novelist and an ex-pupil. Sometimes, in lieu of a supervision, he took me to the pub and then on for a special curry, which led us on to India, to E. M. Forster, the future of the novel, liberals, subversion, homosexuality, the secret society of the Cambridge Apostles (Hugh had been one), communists (Hugh had been one) and spies (could he have been one?). In those beguiling hours it was easy to fall under his spell, and I did. Teaching English is partly about casting spells and telling captivating stories to the young.

'Every great Poet is a Teacher,' Wordsworth wrote to Sir George Beaumont in February 1808, adding, 'I wish either to be considered as a Teacher, or as nothing.' From the first, quoting those words to me, Hugh encouraged me to be a teacher ('You'll be good at it, dear boy') and he also encouraged me to write ('It's like a water-divining stick, you feel the pull, I can tell you do'). Flattery, yes; encouragement, yes.

While he may never have read my undergraduate essays, in later years he certainly read my novels and listened to my radio plays. He wrote to me about the manner in which I moved from the third to the first person within a sentence, and my registers of language. The enduring power of common words fascinated him. He liked the intensely personal way I described the familiar, reminding me yet again that Wordsworth made you sense the complexity of the simple.

I loved it, too, when he came to my school and talked to my classes: he liked the fact that I did both, teach and write. Indeed we were scheduled to broadcast together on the Third

Programme, a two-handed discussion about teaching and writing, when, just before the studio date, he died. In his last visit to my home in 1982 he sat on the bed of my nine-year-old daughter and told her a story. It was strong in narrative surprise, whimsical, slightly shocking and perfectly pitched at her level. I told Hugh I'd never heard the story before.

'I just made it up, dear boy. She seemed to enjoy it. You didn't mind, did you?'

George Watson read, marked and commented on every sentence and every paragraph that I wrote. Here was a contrast indeed! He believed in the discipline of English and could see I needed that rigour brought to my work. If it wasn't a discipline, George argued, what were we reading English at university for, what was the educational, moral and financial justification for English degrees, not to mention all those grants? If an English degree was no more than a random subjective read, a free-for-all, and free from all objective analysis, it had no right to be called a discipline.

In this spirit he rightly insisted upon the weekly reading being done – and took his pen to my work. He cut out unnecessary first paragraphs, put lines through tautologous phrases and savaged sentimentality. He wanted an argument. *This sounds fine, but what does it mean?* An excellent question. He wanted clarity and encouraged lean, crisp prose. My marking as a schoolteacher is precisely modelled on George Watson's example. When I was going through a phase of putting 'learned' footnotes at the bottom of each page of my essay he wrote, 'To think a footnote is a sign of scholarship is a vulgar error.' A Baconian put-down of some beauty.

George Watson expected you to work hard. He expected you to go to lectures and to make the library part of your life. I approved of his expectation. He did not give the time of day to charming evasions, nor did he allow the supervisions to descend into chat; and if they did ever embarrassingly peter out that was because of the thinness of my knowledge. Sometimes what I had written in my essay was the sum total of my grasp. Aware of that, and always concerned for my development, he prompted me at all hours with suggested reading (these hand-written notes arrived in my pigeonhole, a personal touch I greatly appreciated), alerting me to the latest acquisitions, articles or books which had recently arrived in the University Library. I felt I was on the case and ahead of the game. Sometimes, briefly, I even felt I was batting in his league.

Through no fault of George's, this had its drawbacks. I became too dependent, too concerned to find out what this or that scholar had just published, and in no time I had allowed myself to become distracted in a maze of articles (some not worth reading), a replica of Wordsworth's 'floating island', amphibiously drifting, wandering the stacks of the college or the faculty or the university library in a desperate search for knowledge. Far from gaining true insights and knowledge, I now realise I had gone under to second-rate literary criticism.

It was only when I had been teaching for about five years that I gradually shed that mind-set. While explaining things to my pupils I faced the fact that, as an undergraduate, I had not been thinking for myself. I had, while over-keen to be thought academic, slipped away from feeling or writing as honestly as I should have, losing confidence in my own intuitive truths, and in so doing failed to see the big picture. Curiously enough, to see the folly of this all I needed to do as an undergraduate was to reread Wordsworth and apply it to myself, but somehow I did not put the two sides of my life together. I did not see what was under my nose.

Hugh Sykes Davies and George Watson were complementary figures, both kindness itself to me, and at its best my classroom style is a fusion of their two approaches; or at least

I often bounce between the two, the personal and the disciplined.

Unwittingly, in an oblique way, George Watson also set me off on my own writing. When I was in my last year at Cambridge one of George's most influential books, *The Literary Critics*, was published. I was asked to review it for a magazine. A few months later I was eating dinner in St John's (facing the portrait of Wordsworth, 'the bony face', a private game I liked to engineer) when two people opposite, strangers to me, were talking in admiring terms about the review to which only my initials were penned. In their conversation, which filled me with delicious pride, they assumed the review had been written by Dr Stern, later Professor Stern, the distinguished German scholar whose initials were very close to mine. If they thought Dr Stern had written that,

> *then I could write!*
> *We had crossed the Alps!*

Twelve more years passed before I made my first attempt at a novel. It was published. I'm glad I did not rush into writing because I was and still am a slow learner. Throughout my life writing school reports has been for me a regular discipline in thinking about and describing my pupils, trying to put my finger on their strengths, weaknesses and characteristics; and that assessing discipline is not a world away from the character sketches which a dramatist or novelist needs.

By the end of my time at Cambridge – an unremarkable time, no doubt, but however unremarkable we still like to appropriate those seminal three years as 'my time' or 'our time' – I knew I wanted to be a teacher and openly said so. I accepted a job in Scotland. If I wasn't clever enough to be a don, then a schoolteacher it would be. No shame in that: it ran in the family, it was in my blood. I had my models, and even more importantly, I had developed the enduring belief that perception, the art of reading people, lies at the heart of good teaching and good writing.

There have been a number of poems written about Wordsworth. The one by Sidney Keyes I first came across when I was an undergraduate, and I immediately liked it. It was some while before I learnt that Keyes had been a pupil at Tonbridge School, where I have largely spent my life, and over the years this has made the poem still more special to me.

Edward Thomas was killed at Arras in the First World War, Sidney Keyes in the Tunisian campaign in the Second. What a loss was there!

13

William Wordsworth

No room for mourning: he's gone out
Into the noisy glen, or stands between the stones
Of the giant ridge, or you'll hear his shout
Rolling among the screes, he being a boy again.
He'll never fail nor die
And if they laid his bones
In the wet vaults or iron sarcophagi
Of fame, he'd rise at the first summer rain
And stride across the hills to seek
His rest among the broken lands and clouds.
He was a stormy day, a granite peak
Spearing the sky; and look, about its base
Words flower like crocuses in the hanging woods,
Blank though the dalehead and the bony face.

SIDNEY KEYES (1922–43)

14

A Brief Brush With The Real World

When you left my father's primary school at eleven – unless, of course, you were a class traitor (as I was later to be called in the pub) – you either went 'up the road' to Thornbury Grammar School or 'down the road' to Filton High School or 'over the road' to Patchway Secondary School: the road in question being the busy A38 from Bristol to Gloucester. In the early 1960s, when I was on vacation from Cambridge, with comprehensivisation just around the corner, and with my teaching career in Scotland coming up on the horizon, I sometimes went over the road to teach at Patchway Secondary School.

Well, 'teach' not teach.

Nevertheless as it was the first time in my life I had stood in front of a class, it was a big moment. To reach the school, a representative glass palace built in 1952, you dodged the traffic, cut through a potholed transport café car park, passed the sweet shop on the left-hand side of Hempton Lane, and turned into the ninety-five-acre school site which ran down to the railway line and to the famous, though unremarkable, Patchway roundabout. In the 1950s we were always talking about the roundabout. Don't ask me why, but in the 1950s roundabouts were in. And don't ask me why I was asked to help out at Patchway, but I was.

The headmaster, Eric Scarbrough, though I did not know it at the time, was to become my father-in-law. He had built the school, his school, literally from its grass roots, and he remained its first head for twenty-two years. As I have talked about education more to Eric than to anyone else for the last forty years, in describing (for a few pages) what he achieved I am describing things I admire in a teacher and a headmaster. As well as being a personal anecdote, I want to celebrate a particular kind of no-nonsense approach which still holds good.

Though he lived in a very different world from the public school and Cambridge 'world' I had come to know, we met educationally on many points. He told me about the challenges he faced, and asked me about mine. He always wanted me to look around his school, and he always wanted to meet, and (given the chance) to interrogate, any public school colleagues who in later years came to stay with me. He did not see education in political terms of left v. right but as a matter of practical right v. wrong. Indeed, I cannot easily separate my family and my wife's family experiences from my views on teaching. Everything has merged. Many of the methods that I have come to adopt, and many of the beliefs that run in my blood, cut across all the generations and come from every kind of school: primary, secondary, grammar, comprehensive and independent. I am aware of – indeed, curiously proud of – that fortuitous, pragmatic mix.

In August 1952, Eric had been appointed from a mining town in Yorkshire. The school opened with seventeen staff and 421 pupils in January 1953 – not a staff–pupil ratio many heads would enjoy. In the months between his appointment and the school opening he personally supervised every aspect of the building programme, dealt with architects, ordered all the books, furniture and apparatus and worked on the grounds. For over two years he and his family lived in some unused classrooms. (You can't live more over the shop than that.) In a couple of seasons he had also created a cricket field, square and nets: all, sadly, gone to rack and ruin now.

In his first 1953 speech to his staff (for which I have his notes in front of me now) he set out his practical plan. You could never call it a Vision Statement, but *it was him* and it worked. Most schools he had been in recently, he said, had been based on 'starry-eyed theories which may interest some of the staff but which do nothing for the pupils'. Most schools were schools to get out of. This was because they did not make sense. Patchway Secondary School would make sense and be a school to get into. That was the challenge and he and the staff would rise to it. (Eric would almost certainly have agreed with John Passmore who wrote in *The Philosophy of Teaching*, 'The best way of being exciting is to go wildly wrong.')

What did he want? He wanted (and he got) all the best features of other schools, of whatever political persuasion: a house system, prefects, strong pastoral care, streaming, uniform, and daily assemblies with all the staff present in which the school would celebrate the achievements of all its pupils. He wanted no Mondays off for female staff, no smoking, no gimmicks; he would wage war on absenteeism and insist on staff punctuality in lessons as well as pupil punctuality.

All pupils would be encouraged to enjoy singing and drama. If they were shy and inarticulate this form of expression would help. Many young people were handicapped for life by poor speech. All boys and all girls would be encouraged to play games. There would be a fund for those who were unable to pay for their school kit. All teams would play in the school colours.

Not very original? Sounds like a secondary modern school

aping an old-fashioned grammar school? Bit authoritarian in tone, isn't it? Yes, he would reply, and it has stood the test of time. What's wrong with the best aspects of the grammar schools? He had been a pupil at one. Why throw away the good things? He did not believe in throwing the baby out with the bath water. What was wrong with the best things he saw in independent schools? He wanted them, insofar as they could be afforded, in his school. He saw the importance of high expectation, the competitive edge, smart appearance and self-respect. 'It works,' he'd say, 'it works.'

Eric Scarbrough did not need anyone telling him about political pressures from the right or, more pertinently, from the left. Like many a shrewd head, he kept his own politics close to his chest – I'm still not sure what they were – but all his school career (he was head of three schools) he had worked non-stop for those who were not fortunate, those who were not well off and those who had not been selected. He knew and felt deeply all the manifold injustices of education. He knew all about funding, the regional variations in the 11-plus pass rate, transfers, birth-rates, teenage pregnancies, staff shortages in critical subjects (especially in science and mathematics), union troubles, LEAs and NUTs.

He was closely in touch with his community's aspirations yet he kept both feet firmly planted. Eric promised he would set up a school farm, with goats, pigs and poultry. (He did.) In due course he would build a swimming pool. (He did.) He said the academic results would be better for his pupils than anyone would ever have dreamt. (They were.)

The mood of the time was expressed by Anthony Crosland, the public-school-educated Labour Education Secretary, who told his wife that his aim was 'to close every fucking grammar school in the land'. While Eric firmly supported the comprehensive development, and led Patchway fully into that era, he was tough and single-minded in his concerns and as old-fashioned as he was enlightened. He despised fulsome gestures and heady promises.

He warned that with the passing of the 11-plus examination there was a risk that primary school pupils would be less well prepared in the basics; that many bright pupils might not be sufficiently stretched in their time at the comprehensives; that pupils at the top of his 'old' secondary modern might not feel the same pride when finding themselves in the middle of a huge comprehensive; and that comprehensives could never, as was being overconfidently claimed, embrace all that had been best in a grammar school; furthermore, he wondered if abolishing the grammar schools would, ironically, work to the advantage of the independent sector.

All this he was saying in the 1960s and 1970s, but it was not a tune the educational disc jockeys would then play.

Anyway, on my summer vacations from Cambridge, I left behind the world of my university education and crossed the road and cut through the potholed car park and 'taught' at Patchway; and never have the inverted commas around taught been more justified.

Now, though, I saw Eric at first-hand. There he was, hands-on, hawk-eyed, striding up and down the corridors, asking questions, checking up on everyone and, if need be, peering through the glass in the classroom doors. After school, he even checked the lavatories to see the latest graffiti: 'I want to know what they're saying about me, lad.' In a word, he was everywhere.

For years I had known all about state primary schools; now I had the opportunity not only to see real teachers doing the job in a demanding secondary school but to try my hand myself. I took some English lessons. I helped with games. I did a lot of invigilating and I listened in the staff room. This all added up to a bit of teaching experience. It also added up to drinking money.

Before I started Eric gave me his written advice to a new teacher. Here it is:

Cheerful, willing co-operation is won by sympathy, friendliness and tact, but assume from the first moment the authority of your position.

Don't be fussy, dictatorial or pompous, but alert and vigorous. Get to know your pupils as individuals not as units in a class.

Command the class with your eyes. Use your eyes to encourage or to warn. If it is necessary to restrain do so in a way which does not cause resentment.

Dress appropriately. Deal with your pupils with dignity.

Try to inspire.

Quite a tough call, and way beyond me at that stage, but in fact it is very close in every detail to Benson's advice based on his twenty years at Eton: two teachers, from vastly different backgrounds and traditions, but arriving at the same conclusions.

In my classes the boys were tough but the girls were the first to switch off. They made up their faces. In fact they never switched on because I chose inappropriate material and did not know how to hold their attention. I thought I handled this quite well, by trying to appear unrattled, but what I hoped they would see as cool tolerance I suspect they wrote off as weakness. They did not even open their plays, preferring to prop their mirrors against their big handbags and work in great detail on their beehive hair-dos. That I was the son of Mr and Mrs Smith, at whose school some of them had been pupils, could not have mattered less. So what? As far as they were concerned I was a prat. As Edmund Blishen put it in *Roaring Boys*, 'though there was no dreadful disorder there was never much order'.

When the fifteen-year-olds in my classroom were replaced by a class of twelve-year-olds things were only slightly easier. Very slightly and very briefly, because they soon got my number too. Once again Blishen – surely he must have taught at the same school – captured my plight, providing me with the scant comfort that others had been in this predicament before: 'It was as though, fresh from contending with man-eating tigers, I should have taken too light a view of killer ants.' With the twelve-year-olds I tried to appear friendly and in control. That's the decent thing, I thought, but it didn't work. If I protested, they were very good at mock incomprehension, and once or twice I heard a dreadful note of pleading in my voice: the death-knell for a teacher. What saved my bacon with the boys of all ages was that I was a Bristol Rovers fan. Still a prat, but a Bristol Rovers prat. If I'd been a Bristol City prat it really would have been all over.

Day by day I swung between depression and elation. I had enough good moments to think I could more or less make it, moments when I could tell quite a few were listening. Generally speaking I was strong on lively preambles to boring and deteriorating lessons. I did, however, get some excellent writing from a few, and a flow of trust began to develop. Or, at the very least, I would create a brief lull or a temporary peace with a good short story. But I had no steady, daily control. Fortunately I liked the boys and girls, and I think pupils sense that, and fortunately I had my parents to talk to in the evenings.

The parts of my day I liked best were helping with games, talking to pupils around the school, joining in any activity for which another teacher had the final responsibility (i.e. teaching without the nasty bits), and invigilating. In the years since then I have come to loathe invigilating, but on those long, hot days it was a wonderful relief not to be asked to hold a class's attention. While invigilating I could read and dream and watch the flies on the windows and recover my self-respect.

Not many candidates asked for more paper. This was, remember, in the days when an invigilator could slump in his chair with a newspaper and have done with it. A bit of a doddle. Modern invigilating is a nightmare, with different-coloured papers, endless instructions, so many invigilators per pupil, widespread paranoia about cheating (comic, really, when you think of what passes for course work), and with extra areas penned off for dyslexics, claustrophobics and ago-raphobics. It takes real professional skill these days to invigilate without unwittingly calling into play the Health and Safety Act, 1984.

Anyway, on this hot day in 1962 we were in the gym, with all the doors open and the grass being cut noisily outside. (All school groundsmen wait for an examination to start before going berserk on the patch of grass closest to the place of the examination.) Another university student, a comrade in arms, and I were invigilating the English exam. His friendship at school and our hours in the pub each evening helped me to get over my demoralised, jumpy days.

Halfway back in the gym, on the left-hand side, there was a beautiful girl in a white blouse and a maroon skirt. School uniform, regulation blouse, regulation skirt, but there was nothing regulation inside them. She had the most wonderful breasts. As someone who had a full-size true-to-life cut-out of Brigitte Bardot on my bedroom wall I should know. And this girl was no cut-out. She was alive and well.

Anyway, she kept asking for more paper. Ever the profes-sional, I was always there in a flash, and yet I had never noticed in my lessons that creative writing or indeed any kind of writing was her strongest point. In fact she made no attempt even to write on the fresh paper I handed her out. On the third occasion I was leaning over her she whispered:

'Him.'

'Who?' I said.

'Him.' She nodded at my co-invigilator.

'Yes?'

'Tell him something from me.'

'Yes?'

She handed me a folded-over piece of writing.

'Give him this, and tell him from me, if he won't go out with me tonight I'm taking my bra off here and now.'

I bent down, my face close to hers.

'Don't do that,' I whispered. 'Please.'

'I will!'

'I'd be really pleased if you wouldn't.'

(Well, yes and no, yes and no.)

'I will,' she said. 'See if I don't.'

'Right, I'll tell him . . . I'll tell him what you said.'

'You'd better! And give him that.'

'Right. And you'll see him afterwards?'

'Now. I'll see him *now*.'

'*Now?*'

'Or else.'

She undid her top button. God alive!

It sounds like a 'Carry On' film, I know, but that is because it *was* like a 'Carry On' film. I hurried back across the gym and told my friend. He stood up, walked coolly down the aisle, bent down and spoke to her as if he was, for all the world, explaining a problem in the examination paper or clearing up a minor misprint. Then he straightened up and went back to his seat. She caught my eye, mouthed, 'Thanks,' and did up her top button.

15
Fly

A fat fly fuddles for an exit
at the window-pane.
Bluntly, stubbornly, it inspects it,
like a brain
nonplussed by a seemingly simple sentence
in a book
which the glaze of unduly protracted acquaintance
has turned to gobbledygook.

A few inches above where the fly fizzes
a gap of air
waits, but this
has not yet been vouchsafed to the fly.
Only retreat and a loop or swoop of despair
will give it the sky.

CHRISTOPHER REID

16
Finding The Balance

After girls undoing their bras, advocating 'balance' sounds a bit boring. There's something about the sound and the meaning, indeed the very look of the word balance, that makes you want to say, No, thanks, I'd rather spill a bit of blood, where are the machetes, give me a few nutters instead. Being balanced may be admirable and absolutely to the point if you are an accountant or a runner or hitting a golf ball or aiming to be a high-wire artist, but for a creative person or a young teacher setting out on his journey it sounds rather too like Captain Sensible. Even so, my lesson plan – based on my experience in my early years in schools – says, 'Argue the case for a balanced life.'

For a teacher it all starts at the very beginning. When I went into the profession (I started in Scotland in 1964) the unspoken rule in most independent schools was that in term-time you devoted your whole life to the job and that you recovered your health and your sanity in the holidays. In term-time you married the school and in the holidays you had a brief affair with The Real World. This unnaturally neat division may work for some but it did not then, and does not now, work for me. Quite apart from anything else, it makes for bad teaching.

It was only after I had left Loretto (my first post and a school where I learnt a great deal) that I realised I had met almost no one outside the school grounds, that I had buried myself in my job and – most culpably – had seen almost nothing of Edinburgh, a great city not five miles away. It might as well have been five thousand miles. It might as well have been Beirut. True, I sometimes dashed into a restaurant or a film or art gallery or rugby international, but I was only dashing in, never really absorbed or fully enjoying myself. In no time I was working too hard; within a year, despite a most helpful head of department, I had lost my sense of balance. I was 100 per cent for the school and in the school and thinking school. Sometimes, and for no obvious reason, I could find myself in tears.

My first lesson, by the way, which one would have expected to be a Big Life Moment and which I surely ought to remember, I confess I do not. I got so drunk the night before, partly from nerves but mostly from whisky, that by 2 a.m. I was unable to stand up, and I spent my first day in the classroom deep breathing with my head out of the window, unable to eat and only drinking water. The first lesson I learnt in my proper teaching career was, then, to be wary of those who opened a new bottle of whisky and threw the top into the waste-paper basket.

It was also during my first year at Loretto that I first encountered the following: a boy was hovering near the door at the end of a lesson, waiting for everyone to go before he spoke to me. Usually this means the pupil is unhappy or lonely or being bullied. In this case, not so. He walked to my desk, with a shy, embarrassed, smile:

'Do you mind if I ask you something?'

'Of course not, fire away.'

'Well, the thing is, I've been wondering, why are you doing this?'

'I'm sorry?'

'Doing what you're doing.'

'Doing what?'

'Teaching. Why are you teaching? What are you doing here?'

'Do you mean I shouldn't be teaching, that I'm no good, because if so I find that a bit—'

'No, no, sir, I don't mean that, I mean why have you come into teaching? I mean, the thing is, you could be *doing* something with your life.'

'Something *worth* doing, you mean?'

'Yes.'

He was, of course, meaning to be nice, even to be flattering. He wanted to know my answer. He was trying to encourage me. He was saying the big world was out there. Success was out there. Not just The Beatles, Bob Dylan and The Rolling Stones but other people doing Interesting Things with their lives. He saw me as one of those. He could not imagine that anyone could choose to be a teacher, could choose to do something so low in status, when he could have done something else. He could not have known how much this would hurt me, much though I smile at the encounter now. Even so, far from making me ponder over any status I did not have or any financial advantages I did not possess, this conversation made me wonder if perhaps I was becoming dull, not fulfilling my potential as a teacher and as a person: losing my edge, in fact, from overwork. More worrying still, losing touch with myself.

This happens all too easily. Within days of arriving, if not well before the first day of your first term, senior people move in on the new teacher. It happened to me in Scotland. It still happens every day in schools. Not surprisingly, the new teacher is keen to please. Never again in his career will the teacher be more idealistic, more apprehensive, more determined to win approval (or in my case more drunk).

Whatever they may solicitously suggest to you face to face in the job interview about the need to keep a balance in your life, most heads and senior management teams encourage staff, especially young staff, to take on as much as they can and then to take on a little bit more. After all, all the jobs (whether carrying extra pay or – more likely – not) have to be done. Where are the willing hands, paid or unpaid, where are those who will say 'Give me more'? Try the young ones. The management dream scenario is for the staff to be at full stretch, or preferably just over full stretch, without actually snapping. This is sometimes called creative tension.

You are flattered, leant on, charmed, co-opted and thanked. You are told you're very kind if you'd be willing to take on x, y and z. I found myself not only teaching a full timetable but running the 1st XI in cricket, producing the school play, a living-in house tutor and refereeing 1st XV matches. It's not compulsory, of course. Resist, though, and at best you could seem a touch uncommitted or prone to be a moaner or somewhat semi-detached or just a little off-hand, and at worst a bloody idle so-and-so.

Selflessly take on everything, however, tolerate any tedium, say yes of course I will, and you are an impressive young person, a credit to the profession, the sort of person the school is proud to count amongst its own. This is the 'one of us' catch. I wanted to be impressive, I wanted to be a credit to the school, I wanted the school to be proud of me. (I still do.) Say yes and you are smiled upon and nodded about. You have satisfied your hunger for admiration. You are pointed out for future promotion. (If you are selfless but a bit of a plodder, a bit of a donkey, you will simply be used. Frankly you can forget the promotion. Sorry. But, as you are a young teacher, you don't know that yet.) Meanwhile, the easiest way to be accepted and pointed out is to do everything. I did everything, even – God help me – take hockey.

This mind-set afflicts many other professions where it is now sadly rife among my friends and ex-pupils. Work in the year 2000 is now so in, so esteemed, that nobody dares to question it. If there is another view, one does not hear it. The issue has moved way beyond ordinary ambition. Indeed in some of the higher-paid and higher-profile jobs, where money is king, it has become a macho madness, a world where you are encouraged to work all day and every day from dawn until midnight – even Sunday mornings at the office – for the team or profession or business.

How often has one heard, and in what awed tones, how few hours Mrs Thatcher slept – some say five, some say four, wow! – as if that was a central plank of her achievement. Or how tired Mr Blair looks, but he keeps on coming up for more. Wow! Wouldn't you like to be talked about like that? Someone who scythed day after day away in nonstop work? See that man over there, see that woman over there, yes, the one drinking coffee, she never goes to bed before two and she's up before seven. How impressive is *that*!

Hearing such talk, you want to prove that you can take it, you have to show that you are just as tough, that you are on board, that you don't feel the heat, not you, oh no, *you* never crack. You admit that considerable pressure is on you but you admit it in a self-admiring way, it's exciting, it's demanding, yes, but necessary if you and the team are to succeed. If you look as if you are going to buckle, you are weak and should never have been invited into the kitchen. You are so frightened of failure you dare not even contemplate it.

The trouble with all this is that you start off doing the job, and the job ends up doing you. This affects teachers just as much as politicians and businessmen. Your private life, if you ever had one, goes to pieces. Your interior, your other life, atrophies. You stop listening. Success is your new religion. You can't relax and you wonder if you even should. Why aren't you – as you should be – working? You couldn't possibly read a book (I'd love to have the *time* to read), and if you go to the theatre to see the latest Stoppard (and it is lovely, of course, to be able to afford the best seats) you're asleep well before the interval because have you noticed how hot the theatres are these days?

You have moved lock, stock and barrel into The Achievement Society; you have lost your creative hinterland and you didn't even notice it had gone. You have to be seen at your desk, or on the phone or dashing from one place to another. The truth is (and you'll privately admit this to a close friend) you're only happy when you're working. Frankly, you'd rather work than talk to your partner or sort out your children or keep up with your friends. Reflection brings dangerous thoughts. So, back to the desk. Back to the place where you win praise.

Each year you will apologise briefly on your Christmas cards, and promise to do better next year. Where *does* the time go, eh? In one sense, of course, it is a much easier route; if you return to the office or spend all evening marking books or doing admin you are cut off from other demands and distractions. Dammit, you're being good, you're only doing a good job. You can even reproach yourself for ever leaving your desk in the first place. Furthermore, at your desk you're more in control. You are only exposing yourself in areas where you can establish the ground rules and codes of behaviour and perform the way you like to perform.

In the teaching profession, certainly not a profession associated with high pay or expensive theatre seats, slavish overwork is usually a disaster. There are exceptions, those teachers who do nothing but work and still teach each lesson in a highly professional if ashen-faced way, but they are rare and they are not good role models. Most teachers who are wrongly tempted to follow this example of overwork might do an impressive job for the first few weeks of term, living on

high-octane energy and winning accolades for inspiring everyone with their unstinting efforts. Before half-term, however,
they are usually more than half spent; shortly after that they
are exhausted, and the last third of term they are self-pitying,
burnt-out cases.

That's bad enough. But they are so overworked they very
soon become censoriously resentful: 'I'm doing bloody everything.' That self-assessment is not only very wide of the mark,
it is an approach as inefficient as it is unprofessional. In far too
many schools and classrooms, teachers are going through the
motions for the final month. Any buzzy impression made in
the early weeks is long forgotten and more than cancelled
out. The pupil is sold short.

If you turn up to class each day so exhausted and low that
you cannot raise the game, you have fallen at the first fence.
However many ticks you have in other boxes, you have failed
in your central purpose. A banker or politician or solicitor or
businessman (or those in any number of jobs) may be able to
work cripplingly long hours, and no doubt they have many
pressures on them of which my profession knows little, but
they do not have to keep acting, performing, and transferring
energy to an audience of young and demanding pupils who
change every forty minutes. That is the daily challenge for a
teacher, and it must be met.

If they are to do this at all well, teachers need to 'look after
themselves'. Usually that colloquial phrase carries a satirical or
pejorative edge, suggesting that the person who looks after
himself in effect is doing the bare minimum and doing that
bare minimum in a self-interested way. I am using the phrase
absolutely straight. This is not an essay in praise of idleness
and easy riders (about which George Watson has written so
wittily), but an argument based on the conviction that a
teacher cannot work flat-out all term in the mistaken belief
that he can spend the whole holiday recovering.

Real discipline, I would argue, is not always a matter of driving yourself on; real discipline is also knowing when to stop. This goes for all people in all jobs. Certainly, as a teacher you need to pace yourself, to sense when you're losing your perspective, to recover as you go along, to have some fun and relaxation in the term-time, to think of other things, to enjoy yourself and not to fall into a puritanically self-obsessed rut. And for their part, the holidays are much more rewarding and memorable if there is some intellectual challenge and creative reflection. Wordsworth called this 'a wise passiveness'.

For a teacher and for a parent finding that delicate balance – or getting a life – is a tricky business.

17
The Price We Pay

WALTER (*seizing on this minute encouragement*): Vic, I
wish we could talk for weeks, there's so much I want to
tell you . . . (*It is not rolling quite the way he would wish
and he must pick examples of his new feelings out of the
air.*) I never had friends – you probably know that. But
I do now, I have good friends. (*He moves, sitting nearer
Victor, his enthusiasm flowing.*) It all happens so gradually. You start out wanting to be the best, and there's
no question that you do need a certain fanaticism;
there's so much to know and so little time. Until
you've eliminated everything extraneous – (*he smiles*) –
including people. And of course the time comes when
you realise that you haven't merely been specialising
in something – something has been specialising in you.
You become a kind of instrument, an instrument that
cuts money out of people, or fame out of the world.
And it finally makes you stupid. Power can do that.
You get to think that because you can frighten people
they love you. Even that you love them. And the
whole thing comes down to fear. One night I found
myself in the middle of the living room, dead drunk
with a knife in my hand, getting ready to kill my wife.

ESTHER: Good Lord!

WALTER: Oh ya – and I nearly made it too! (*He laughs.*) But there's one virtue in going nuts – provided you survive, of course. You get to see the terror – not the screaming kind, but the slow, daily fear you call ambition, and cautiousness, and piling up the money.

ARTHUR MILLER, The Price

18
Some Simple Dodges

Beyond needing 'half an hour' to tell a new young teacher at Eton 'the simple dodges which have proved in my own case useful and effective' A. C. Benson was sceptical about the training of teachers. He did not believe it could be learnt by demonstration, nor that you could form yourself on a model.

While I instinctively line up with the sceptics, as a father and a teacher I do (as a previous chapter showed) believe in models; I do believe in watching others, in listening to gifted performers and in nicking the best habits and tricks I see in other classrooms and in other schools. In their worlds, painters, sportsmen, musicians and actors do the same.

Ever since I arrived (perhaps just a little more balanced?) in Tonbridge in 1967 I have been trying to come to terms with the demands of what I do. Every school I visit in this country and abroad (and I visit many) is also a learning experience. I have no ideology. I see my job in very simple, human, practical and often psychological terms, yet the simple dodges I describe in the following pages have taken me half a lifetime to learn. Some of them came easily, some I learnt the hard way. I see them more as life-lessons than as a coherent educational theory; and they could be applied, I think, by anyone who is often in contact with children. This time I will list them, a bit like a hand-out in class.

1. If you have *the power of analogy* you have every chance of being good at the teaching game. 'Good at the game', there I go . . . Good at the game is a revealing metaphor for me because I see playfulness as an essential part of being a parent and being a teacher, and I most often use sporting metaphors to convey ideas or to explain concepts which my pupils may be finding difficult. Such analogies come easily to me as I enjoy watching sport. They also come readily to me from the world of painting, music and film. I often hear myself talking in terms of pitch, texture, direct hits, near misses, goals, winners, tight situations, slow fades, crisp interpassing, free running moments, focus and frames. After using an analogy you sometimes notice your pupils nodding. What, you mean, it's *that* simple?

If you've seen the film *The Full Monty* you may remember the moment when Tom Wilkinson is trying to teach his class of strippers a step in a dance (a step so simple to him, yet so maddeningly difficult to them: a common experience for a teacher) and he suddenly explains it by analogy to the Arsenal off-side trap. Arms up, all move forward together. It dawns. They smile. Like *this*, you mean? And they all move perfectly in time. *Yes, now you've got it.* It's a lovely teaching moment. (Of course, you're far more likely to be able to play the game if you have a life outside school, if you're alive and naturally share some worlds with your pupils – an issue to which I will return.)

Teachers who enjoy analogies tend also to enjoy diversion and may well be prone to take short cuts. They may well be easily bored. All very annoying for the puritans in the staff room, but they do know how to hold the class and they do get across the essentials. Benson reserves one of his great sentences for these: 'A brisk, idle man, with a knack of exposition and the art of clear statement, can be a scandalously effective teacher.' Wonderful use of 'scandalously'.

2. In a lesson – as in a good conversation, as indeed in life – *you need to be light on your feet*, to know when to change gear, when to change the angles and when to change the tone. It helps to have a back-up plan, a lighter or different fall-back idea. You have to be able to alter your response; to know when to stop eye contact, when to let someone else take centre stage, when to disengage or to suggest that enough is enough on a particular topic. You need to know when to talk and when to listen. Many teachers talk too much and listen too little. Some teachers listen to too much waffle and don't cut in enough. The trick is to know which is which.

It isn't enough to be endlessly kind, wonderfully understanding and superhumanly patient. You can be sympathetic too long. Sometimes you need an edge of intolerance, to be a bit of a bastard, otherwise everyone around you takes you for granted. Once they take you for granted, the edge goes. Give them a jolt sometimes. You don't have to be a bastard to teach, far from it, but saintliness is saintliness, and a classroom is not its best setting.

One morning the jolt in my lesson came from an unexpected intrusion. A young colleague of mine, an unconventional and abrasive personality, burst into my classroom. We were reading a play. He didn't knock, he just stormed up to my desk and began to shout at me. I backed away. He followed me, pointing his finger at me. I asked him to calm down, to control himself, couldn't he see I was teaching, we'd talk about it later . . .

'Don't try to humour me!' he shouted. 'I'm fed up with you, fed up with this school, fed up with everything. You make me sick. *The whole place makes me sick!*'

He pointed at my posters, at my photos, said they were all

pretentious rubbish, and so were my views: I talked rubbish and, what's more, I couldn't teach for toffee. Then he stormed out, pausing only to bang on the door from the outside and scream at me again. I sat in my chair. There was a long, ghastly silence. After a few more moments I stood up.

'I'm sorry,' I said to my class, 'I've never had anything like that before . . . I'll have to sort it out . . . I don't know what to say. Did that really happen?'

The class looked at me. Most were shocked and deeply embarrassed.

'It would really help me,' I said, 'the more I think about this, if you wouldn't mind writing down what you just saw and heard. If this turns into something more, I would like some evidence, some witnesses.'

'It was amazing,' one boy said. 'Unbelievable.'

'What did you do to him?' another boy asked.

'Nothing . . . nothing at all. That's why I want you to write down what you saw and heard. You all saw it. Just write it down, would you, word for word, in simple English.'

They all agreed. At the end of a very quiet lesson they handed in what they had written and trooped off. I left the room, head down. A few watched me go down the corridor.

The next time I met that class, the other master and I went in together. My colleague explained that what happened had all been his idea, a put-up job, to see just how much agreement there was over exactly what they had seen, heard and observed. He and I had often, he told the class, disagreed about the value and reliability of eye-witness accounts of a crime. Could you believe what people swore they saw? We all thought we saw the world as it was, but what was the reality, what was the truth?

So, we took it in turn to read out to the class their accounts of his verbal assault on me. It was a terrific forty minutes. Their descriptions were so varied, so disturbingly different, so contradictory and so funny that we all spent most of the time helpless with laughter. As for the next fortnight's work, that was suddenly given to me: we would talk and write on truth, fiction, lies, selective vision, subjectivity and objectivity, and try to see where any clear or subtle lines might be drawn. A murky and fascinating topic. It proved easily the best writing they produced that year.

All that came from a casual moment over lunch with a lively teacher, a teacher who was prepared to run with a risky idea. Normally I would never think of doing such a thing – I've never been comfortable with practical jokes – though this one certainly lifted the level of my teaching. That colleague left the profession, I'm sad to say, even though he had compelling enthusiasm and a great instinct for what made the young tick. He left because, as came out unconsciously in his role play, 'the school made him sick'. Increasingly he felt more on the side of the pupils and less on the side of the staff. Seeing our profession in those terms is a sad oversimplification but you can, under the everyday stresses and expectations of the job – and without realising it is happening to you – lose your balance and become embattled. For some idealistic teachers it can easily become an Us v. Them, the liberals against the establishment. Then everyone loses.

When they themselves were pupils at school some of the best teachers I've worked with were rogues or rebels – as indeed, on one level, they remain at heart. That is a different matter. Because they know a bit more about the world, because they know what it is to have been naughty, because they have subversive feelings (or some sympathy with those who do), they are naturally more able to reach their pupils. Prigs, though they all too often hold court in common room armchairs, are all too often dreary teachers.

3. *Self-mockery helps.* Prigs wouldn't spot self-mockery if it

jumped out of the mirror and smacked them. It is natural for pupils to resist seriousness, and while I can think of a few solemn people who have made reasonably competent teachers, it really is only a few. How do you feel when a solemn-faced vicar walks up into the pulpit? Oh, this is going to be good?

Playfulness and lightness of touch are as important as intellectual passion. A friend, an inspiring teacher, describes his classroom method as 'laugh and learn', and his results are plain to see: they love his lessons and fly through examinations. I try to build self-deflation into my register, playing off the serious subject matter with the undercutting, earthy asides favoured by some characters in Aristophanes and Shakespeare. Deflate rather than inflate yourself, build in a jeer from the crowd, anticipate their objections and you are part of the way to overcoming their natural boredom.

Putting it another way, it is a helpful thing (as A. C. Benson wisely points out) if a teacher is easily bored himself. Some of the best teachers have this lazy side, and in most staff meetings I've noticed they tend to be the first to switch off. They make something of a point of not taking everything too seriously.

When I was teaching at Loretto in Scotland our staff meetings were dire. For some reason they took place in a half-lit drab classroom. A friend of mine, a gifted maths teacher, spent every minute of these interminable events with two stopwatches at the ready. He saw the meetings not as professional gatherings where issues were openly discussed, which they never were, but as material for research. He timed exactly how long each teacher spoke, leaving out only those who made the briefest interjections. The next day he would send me a detailed breakdown of the total contributions in minutes and seconds made by each member of staff. The point he was privately keen to prove was that the length of the teacher's contribution was in inverse proportion to his value to the school community.

I have to say the evidence was compelling.

4. *Put yourself in your pupils' shoes*. The same advice could, I think, be given to parents as well as teachers. How much of all this would you want to listen to? Are you boring the backside off them? Be brisk and lively rather than heavy-handed. How much heaviness can a child take? Family or classroom, in a sense it's the same thing. If you're not too heavy all the time the young will be more likely to join a teacher or a parent in an interesting exchange of views or on an intellectually sharp journey or on an exploration of the big moral issues. Overplay the high moral ground and they're less likely to listen. When teachers strike a certain note we all remember or know the feeling: oh no, he's off again. Benson said that one of his Eton colleagues always talked to his pupils as if he were halfway up the Matterhorn. (I have met them, too, oh I have met them. Bring on the avalanche.)

You could of course argue that 'the brisk, idle man' would be an even better teacher if he was always prepared and never hung-over, but I wouldn't bet on it. You have to accept the whole picture; you don't get ticks in all the boxes. The point is he isn't boring, and it's the boring teachers we want out of the classroom. At least the boring pupils have an excuse: they do not choose to be there.

5. *Do not stand on your dignity*. Sadly, many wonderfully committed teachers drive themselves further and further away from their pupils by working harder and harder. It's a cruel paradox. With the best will in the world the job, as I explained earlier, becomes everything to them. They go under. They feel resentful. They feel undervalued. They become ever more conscious of their position and status (never a hit with the

young), more po-faced, more proud of their service and self-sacrifice, and – worst of all – more tired. Schools come to rely on such teachers. Schools come to use such teachers.

Tiredness can, perversely, even seem an achievement. These tired colleagues are invariably excellent, selfless people. When I am being honest I want to say to them (and I want to say to myself when I can see I am being dragged down that path), 'Don't spend any more time on that. Don't add up any more marks. Don't fill in any more forms. Don't run backwards and forwards between every building as if there's a nuclear attack. Don't photocopy any more paper. You are not teaching better by going on like this, you are teaching worse. Who wants to be taught by anyone in your present state? Go to a film, read a book, go out for a meal. Be with friends. Stay alive.'

Though the professional mind-set encouraged by GCSE and A level has become increasingly dreary, and though form-filling, league tables, course work and modules have in recent years made matters much worse, there's nothing particularly new about all this. In 1902 A. C. Benson warned his profession:

> It is not a self-indulgence, but a plain duty, for teachers to keep themselves fresh and active-minded; and the spirit in which a teacher allows himself to be carried helplessly down a stream of mechanical duties is not only not praiseworthy, but highly reprehensible.

Teachers who work themselves to death, some of them my close friends and colleagues, will be irritated by Benson's words, but the words remain true.

19
Love And Work

The fact is, this work is as dreary as shit.
I do not like it a bit.
While at it I wander off into a dream.
When I return, I scream.

If I had a lover
I'd bear it all, because when day is over
I could go home and find peace in bed.
Instead

The boredom pulps my brain
And there's nothing at day's end to help assuage the pain.
I am alone, as I have usually been.
The lawn is green.

The robin hops into the sprinkler's spray.
Day after day
I fill the feeder with bird-seed,
My one good deed.

Night after night
I turn off the porch light, the kitchen light.
The weight lodged in my spirit will not go
For years, I know.

There is so much to do
There isn't time for feeling blue.
There isn't any point in feeling sad.
Things could be worse. Right now they're only bad.

VIKRAM SETH

20

Gurus, Good And Bad

I went into teaching because I wanted to influence the young. And there's no better reason. I went into it because I believed I could turn them on to my subject, I went into it determined they would enjoy my classes, and – yes, let's be honest, because there is a competitive side – I hoped that my pupils would be more successful with me than they would have been with other teachers.

It's not quite as crude as that sounds, but you quickly come to feel that your classes are 'your' classes, and that 'your' house or team, 'your' orchestra or cast, 'your' lot' is all the stronger for its association with you. You would deny it, of course, and with colleagues you'd talk about the virtues of collaboration and doing the best for everyone in your care and how we're all working towards a common goal, but sneakily you like to think that there is something a bit special about those lucky enough to be with you. You live in the hope, no, you live in the belief that something will rub off on them – which must mean, under the mock modesty, that you have something pretty special to give.

For teachers – or parents, for that matter – who have any charisma there are, however, some real dangers. The young are very susceptible, especially to strong, compelling personalities with a gift for exposition, and teachers know, recognise and enjoy the buzz they feel when they see young, innocent, even not-so-innocent but attentive faces, pupils who are lapping it up and want more. It is not all that difficult to feel you're an intellectual leader, if not a cultural leader, if not a spiritual influence. It's heady stuff. That's part of the thrill of the job, if not *the* thrill. We sense we can mould and shape our pupils: our pupils are special because they listen, and they don't listen to just any old teacher. Oh, no. They're far too discriminating for that. They listen *to me*.

There is a very short list of books every teacher should read (and a very long list – many to be found under the heading 'Gender and Management Studies' – which every teacher should avoid) and Anthony Storr's stand high in the first category. I have already briefly mentioned Storr's *Psychotherapy*, but two other works of his, *Solitude* and *Feet of Clay*, have made me think more carefully, and behave more cautiously, in this central, yet controversial sphere: a teacher's real or potential power to influence.

Solitude, originally entitled *The School of Genius*, is not – on a first reading – concerned with teaching as such, but on the deepest level it goes to the core of my concerns. Throughout my career, and increasingly in the last ten years, the emphasis has been laid on two issues: examination success and the happiness of the pupils in the school. The first is ruthlessly pursued and yet the second is held to be our equal purpose and goal. Are the pupils enjoying it, are they happy (whatever that means), are they popular with their peers, are they all getting on well with each other? Do they relate well to their teachers?

Storr challenges this common twentieth-century assumption that close personal ties are the only source of happiness. By way of exploring the nature of creativity in its highest forms, he looks at case studies of the world's greatest artists and thinkers, and faces up to the evidence that genius is most significantly found in unresolved people. In other words, the social virtues of excellent interpersonal ties, the psychotherapist's working rule that it would be a healthy thing if we were all well adjusted and sorted, may be a goal sought at the risk of closing down the school of genius.

Now, I am not of course saying that schools are full of geniuses, or that we should treat all our classes as if they were. Nor am I suggesting that the school prospectus should have as its vision statement the determination to turn out wonderfully unresolved people. Even though we have all too many schools claiming to be The School For The Family, I still can't see The School For The Unhappy catching on. But I have found that many of the most interesting pupils I have taught are angular; they're not easy or chummy. They may well not get on all that well with their peers, and may well not be particularly keen to get on with you. I don't blame them: often I don't get on with myself.

Quite a few of the most thoughtful and sensitive also like to be left alone, or at least left more to themselves; they don't want always to be brought into the circle. These pupils can wrongly be written off as arrogant. Indeed in staff rooms clever pupils are in danger of being written off as arrogant mainly because they don't sit there nodding all the time while some teacher who bores for England is banging on.

Yet many charismatic teachers run their every class on the basis of wanting to be liked, of requiring rapt attention, of achieving impact, of receiving approved wide-eyed wonder. Storr has led me to become suspicious of all that. It often leads to a cult of personality and to the death of thought.

Great fulfilment, Storr explains, can come from solitude. How often do we now ever build such an idea into our teaching day, let alone into our philosophy? Quiet, attentive reading is out; zap zap is in. Being sociable and friendly is the name of the game. Getting on with everyone and being nice to people is not, however, everything: all virtue, as Philip Larkin points out so succinctly in his poem 'Vers de Société', is not social. Many social occasions are little more than empty time-filling, and it is often with a sense of emptiness that one is left.

Nor is the warmth of the teacher–pupil relationship, helpful though it may be, everything. I would put mutual respect far ahead of what currently passes for warmth. I would far rather hear that a teacher is considered a little unapproachable than that he is a popular guy who never sets work, indiscriminately tells all his pupils they're wonderful and gives them all inflated grades. That is a cheap, and increasingly crowded, road. Such teachers base their lives on wanting to be loved, and in so doing sell their pupils short.

A teacher can do a great deal, a very great deal – dammit, he can change lives – but, however compelling he is, however successful in gaining examination results or in establishing rapport, he must keep his feet on the ground, keep a little detachment and never for one moment imagine he is indispensable. The trick for the teacher, and it is the trickiest aspect of a tricky business, is to be involved in an unobtrusively caring and very professional way, while also taking care to keep a part of himself to himself. That way his pupils learn, and that way they learn to leave: to become independent.

Solitude warned me against too readily idealising the lasting effect of a teacher's involvement and it warned me against sentimentality. It made me rethink the complex responsibility of how best to influence difficult and creative pupils – each of whom is very individual – and, perhaps most significantly, it made me confront the discordant elements in myself. If, as a teacher, I am too concerned about fitting into my own community, if I am too hand-in-glove, if I am all things to all men, how can I stay true to myself and reach those who are not like that? Because *I* am not like that.

Solitude made me think. Solitude does make you think.

There are, thank goodness, no schools for gurus. In an equally fascinating, later book, *Feet of Clay*, Storr looks at gurus, good gurus, bad gurus and gurus who slide over the line from being one to the other. He comes to terms with dreadful monsters like David Koresh and Jim Jones; he examines the claims of Jung and Freud; and he moves upwards to one of the greatest saints, Ignatius of Loyola, and to Jesus Christ. It is a disturbing journey from unworthy, self-deluded psychopaths to figures who have transformed our vision of life. No teacher can read *Feet of Clay* without a chill.

Dictators, spiritual gurus, priests and teachers have a tendency to tell others how to live. Telling other people how to think and behave and live can be a drug. I am well aware of that even as I write this book. You can't get enough of being listened to and those who listen often come to be followers. Sometimes, when I sense I am being listened to almost too intently, I break off eye-contact and change track. I hear a warning bell, a warning voice: 'Beware thy follower.' A teacher can spend all day on this territory.

Indeed, I have lost count of the teachers I've worked with who have shown not only a worrying lack of balance but dangerously guru tendencies. They arrive full of enthusiasm, full of that youthful idealism which is at first so inspiring and which can make older teachers feel (resentfully) that they have lost it. They arrive claiming to love their pupils, and they claim it often; they work night and day; they have what one old cynic used to call a 'Jesus Christ complex'; they sometimes even start to look a little like stereotypes of Jesus. Nothing is too much bother if it is for their pupils. They claim their pupils are fantastic. The pupils claim the teacher is fantastic. If any pupil becomes disillusioned, however, or fails to fall under the spell, the guru teacher can swiftly become nasty in exercising his authority.

All too soon such guru teachers find the school in general a rather bleak place, a community unwilling to change and sadly short of soul. Convinced of the power of their own soul and their own specialness, convinced that theirs is the only form of democracy, they soon become intolerant of criticism and see anything which gets in their way as personally hostile. From then on it is usually downhill all the way – either to a quick departure, full of recriminations, or to some kind of breakdown. They don't last.

If you spot a mixture of the self-absorbed and the authoritarian in an otherwise promising teacher, the alarm bells should ring. It may be a case of a good appointment going badly wrong. Most good teachers have a sense of humour, a sense of self-mockery and a healthy realism about the young. All good teachers have the ability to keep running. Most guru-teachers are sprinters: they sentimentalise the young, they're into quick glamour, and they divide the world into 'us' and 'them'. Invariably they are up themselves, and that is where they should stay: where they are no danger to anyone else.

All this can be seen in the much-acclaimed and very bad film *Dead Poets Society*. When I first sat through it, wincing and squirming, I was disturbed to notice so many people in the cinema moved. In the following months others told me how sympathetic and passionate the story was, and how refreshing it had been to see a film on the side of the young; I have even heard good teachers described as 'like Robin Williams in that film'. Anxious that I had not been defensive, or had over-reacted because I felt uncomfortably threatened by the story, I have recently rented the video and watched it again. It was even worse.

For those who have not seen the film – which is set in the late 1950s, when I was in the sixth form – I will briefly summarise the story. An inspirational English teacher, John Keating (played by Robin Williams), returns to his old school in Vermont. Finding the establishment authoritarian and repressive, he encourages his pupils to question conventional views, to seize the day, to stand on their desks and to do their own thing. He even teaches them a Latin tag, Horace's *carpe diem*. (Enjoy today, trust little in tomorrow. Make hay . . . a hazy notion which usually means watch out, girls.)

He wants to take them on a journey of self-discovery. As part of his strategy to change lives he resuscitates the meetings of a society he founded years ago when he himself was a pupil there, the Dead Poets Society. Because he can't get enough of being listened to, for the society meetings he even extends the school hours: these self-conscious and incoherent get-togethers take place at night in a campus cave, where the rapt class swap random lines of poetry and prose (Herrick, Whitman, Thoreau and Tennyson) while he relives his own youth through them. This is freedom. True, there's a lot of personality and not much thought, but, hey, it's great. Sure, the pupils don't learn much about literature, but they do love Robin. (Watch out, boys and girls, I wanted to shout, watch out!)

One impressionable follower, a member of the society, has a very dominating father who wants him to become a doctor. The boy wants to become an actor. The father forbids him to go on the stage. Unable to face the conflict, the boy kills himself. So what are we saying here: that the good die young, while the repressed and the authoritarian old live on? Given this, the English teacher could not expect to last long in his job. When he is dismissed, the pupils stand on their desks in protest.

Far from exploring the fascinating question of what complex and dangerous motives drive a gifted and irresponsible guru figure, this cheap film (along with the pupils) gives the culpable man a standing ovation. Anyone can be a popular teacher for a short time. Anyone with a gift for intimacy can be easily loved. Instead of showing how careful you have to be with youthful idealism this film joins in the cult. It manipulates response and panders to its audience in precisely the same way that Robin Williams panders to his class. Rather than see this irresponsible film, teachers and parents should read Anthony Storr.

21
From Form Photograph

In his introduction to his collection *FORM PHOTOGRAPH* (1971) Stanley Cook – a teacher, lecturer and poet – wrote, 'I like to feel that I have been as practical and unsentimental with a poem as if I had farmed, smithed or carpentered it – that the rest of the family would think I had done some "real work" and had not let them down.' Here are three of his thirty portraits, each beautifully drawn from life: I can see these boys.

(i)   *A little nose like an inverted comma*
     And mousy hair of course, a boy left over
     From an elder brother who captained the First Eleven
     And the School. Looking abstract and remote
     In a saintly way but really rather deaf,
     He passes by the mischief of other boys
     Like an accident; he blinks at a rebuke.
     No pin-ups inside his desk but books as neat
     As biscuits in a packet. Ought I to wish
     For his own sake that he was sometimes insolent?

(ii)   *His spelling is bad to the point of originality*
       And through his accent I hear his father swear
       In the foundry. I scrape him what marks I can
       From the ungrammatical unpunctuated chat
       Of his compositions. Thank heaven that he,
       The biggest and strongest boy in the form,
       Is on my side, calculating the right
       By a one-times table. Had he been born in time
       His bones would lie embedded on the Somme
       As his ancestors' are, form vice-captain and hero.

(iii) *Unhealthily pale as if he were grown indoors*
       Or underneath a brick that excluded the sun,
       He fainted last week in Biology
       At the mention of blood. His mind clicks slowly
       As an automatic telephone exchange
       And prints his pale face with understanding.
       An academic type, still as a stone,
       He likes to think and never meant harm to anyone.

22

Why Winners Come Second

Bad gurus, like bad teachers, have to come first. They won't tolerate anything else. If they could only observe those in their care as closely as Stanley Cook; if they could only step outside their self-absorption and watch good parents at play, they would learn the right approach. When I became a father in the 1970s I found myself watching not only my own pupils but also other families much more.

If you watch a game of cricket on the beach, or a father and son kicking a football against a garage door, or families playing cards or computer games at home, or the whole family racing in a line across the park, or a mother and daughter swimming in the pool – in all of these challenges and competitions not only will you see parents and children having fun, you also see parents coming second. More often than not, the child is allowed to win. The father misses the only straight ball bowled, the mother tires just before the end of the swim, and the young boy's wicked kick curls tantalisingly out of reach and hits just below the chalk line on the garage door. It's a goal! It is indeed. The triumph and self-esteem on the child's face brings a smile to the passer-by.

To say self-esteem is critical in a child's development is a truism, yet the force of this obvious truth is often diminished or forgotten in the later stages of school life. All those parents playing with their young children are doing a good, encouraging job as teachers. Teachers should do the same, even when the adolescents in their classes have lost some of that innocent attraction. True, rather than playing with a few children of his own, a teacher may well have over a hundred pupils coming in and out his room every week, and some of that hundred will be intractable; true, as the pupils go up the school the tactics have to become more subtle, the strategies more varied, the game more complex, but the essential point and goal remain the same: build them up. Give them a taste of winning, of succeeding, of celebrating.

Building them up is not the same thing as filling them with hot air, though there are attendant risks. If a child thinks life is all about winning, or that winning is too easy, there are real shocks ahead. Life can be awful. You don't want children growing up in cloud-cuckoo-land. So you also have to prepare them for disappointment and help them to accept losing, which is an argument often put for competitive games.

But even with the risks, I think a little too much praise, even a little bullshit, does less damage than a continual pouring of cold water. Flatter them, don't flatten them. Both at school and at university I was inspired by teachers who, I later realised, partly flattered me into thinking I was on my way to becoming a scholar. That sharpened my ambition and put a spring into my step. In that hope, I worked ever harder. While I never became a scholar in any sense of the word that matters, I certainly travelled along that path.

It is, furthermore, much easier for a parent or a teacher to pull an overtalkative or bumptious child down a peg than to make someone of low self-esteem believe in himself. It took me too long to work this one out. If a pupil has, say, produced three consecutive pieces of good work, or if you have found reasons to praise, there is a basis of confidence building in him which allows you to move in hard on sloppy or arrogant or casual efforts. The pupil can take it, and in the future may take less for granted. By criticising his work you are showing him respect, the respect of taking his work seriously.

When I inherit a class at the beginning of a school year I no longer want to know how well or badly those pupils have done in earlier terms or years. I would now prefer not to have my ear bent by a teacher telling me how this or that someone is. There are always teachers ready to warn you against a class or individual. I do not want to know the baggage my pupils carry, whether they are thought to be disruptive or under-achievers or lazy, and above all I do not want to know what their IQs are. I have a particular distaste for those most mis-leading numbers. I can think of plenty of show-ponies with high IQs who have never run a good race, and I can think of plenty of diffident or late developers, with moderate IQs, who have accelerated down the final furlongs to take the academic world by storm. All the necessary information and background on offer is only likely to make me pre-judge a pupil. As far as is possible – you can never, of course, com-pletely escape staff room chat – I like all those in my classes to start the first lesson with a clean sheet. I expect well of them all.

Let me flesh this point out by describing a colleague who for many years inspired me with his approach. He taught physics successfully at all levels, though in his own school and university days he had a modest academic record. Seen purely in those A level and final degree terms, his CV was not outstanding. Many heads would, to their great loss, not even have put him on the short list for a job. He was, however, con-sistently effective in the classroom, loved and respected by his pupils and greatly admired by his cleverer colleagues. What were his gifts?

He spoke confidently and naturally, 'with a knack of exposition' – in Benson's telling phrase – 'and the art of clear statement'. He understood that they might not understand, so, if need be, he repeated himself: with no scorn and with even more clarity. Even more significantly, he established an ethos of expectation, a whole class ethos of expectation. It was not the case that only the able pupils would shine. His whole class would do well. That was his intention. That was his style and his expectation. He treated them as if they would do well and there was no reason he could see, if they worked and asked and listened, why they should not. He looked at them openly, with warmth, without irony, with humour, and (though he may not have gone along with my metaphor) he knew how to come second.

Interestingly, he also loved playing sport with and against the boys, where he was most noted for his whole-hearted and unstinted effort. He never stopped trying and he did not mind his open striving being seen. Not for him the effortless superiority or casual display of languid skills. That was not his way: he came off covered in mud and grinning. He ran and bowled till he dropped, but never took it too seriously. In his classroom his pupils felt their muscles, their own intellectual muscles, and developed them. They never stopped trying either.

Every day I walked past his classroom. When I could I had a quick glance in. (By the way, he always arrived in class on time and taught the full forty minutes: a simple discipline which many loose, corridor-chatty teachers might copy.) There he was, jacket off, standing up, looking into their eyes, talking to them all, doing what he called 'a spot of whole class teaching'. A bit of charisma and a lot of dogged, caring determination to get it right.

I found myself walking away, nodding to myself. Here was a daily master class for me. Teachers should take no pleasure in hitting easy winners. Following his example, I tried even harder in my classes to develop not only their intellectual and their imaginative muscles but also their determination to be the very best they could be. I talked to my classes more openly. Out of class I talked to them more individually. When they wrote creatively or read quietly, I decided to do the same and *not* to use that time to do a bit of tidying up, marking or admin. When I was in the classroom my time was their time. (I have since been told by ex-pupils that they liked it not only when I read stories to them but when they could see I was myself lost in a novel during a class reading period. We catch interests and habits from each other.)

By contrast, take the teacher who is always complaining: who always seems to have difficult classes, who always finds they know nothing, who each year finds his pupils even more stupid than last, who comes in to lunch to tell you triumphantly that the best mark in the simple test he's just given them was sixty, '*Sixty! What is the point in me going on?*' (good point), that they arrive at school knowing less and leave knowing less . . . What fun it must be in his lesson! When you read out the timetable (who's teaching who) at the beginning of the year you can't miss the groans when certain teachers are assigned to their set. One boy banged his head hard on the desk:

'Oh *no*! That's *it*! I've got no chance!'

Even if running second can be seen, on one level, as an indulgence or as patronising, it is an indulgence with a higher purpose. Done in the right spirit it works and it does not demean. It is not giving in. It is effective and with experience you can raise the stakes a little more each time. This teaching strategy stretches the pupil's mind, as much as it stretches the athlete's body. It's all part of his warm-up for life. It is a thrill to see what it can do for your own child and for your own pupils.

Indeed, is it so different for adults? In adult friendships and marriages? One partner may already be on the finishing line of any conversation or issue, even before the race is run, yet knows it is important to run together with his friend or part-ner round that track, running with each other and for each other. You have to listen a lot in friendships and in marriage, and then listen again, listen as if it is all new, taking a back seat, resisting the urge to short-cut the whole thing by saying 'Look, the answer to all this is very simple . . .'

You could call this tact, love and decency, but there is an extent to which successful relationships, relationships involv-ing shared growth, are based on a measure of deceit and the rhetoric of equality. In many there is a power imbalance. For teachers the question must be, do you make your pupils more than you damage them? In crude terms, are you a net gain for them? In this challenge you can achieve a great deal by the way you read their needs, the way you listen and the skill with which you run second: in a sense, you develop your pupils partly by your body language.

The opposite temptation is the one teachers should resist, and the one to which many intellectually clever teachers fall: the temptation to dominate most discussions. To show off, to dazzle the class, to be the fastest gun in the west, speaking at top speed, leaving them gasping. In most aca-demic discourse any competent teacher is likely to have more information at his fingertips than even his best pupils. He is also likely to have considered most of the challenging ques-tions in his subject many times. And so, as a teacher, he damn well should have done! But knowing a good deal, and having your back pocket packed with intellectual currency, is not the same as knowing all the answers in an off-putting way. Who likes people bragging about their material or intel-lectual capital?

The point is to leave the classroom not with your overawed

pupils thinking you are brilliant, but with your pupils thinking the subject is fascinating and they are getting somewhere. They must want to return. The trick is that they should want to tell you and to share with you what they have just found out and now feel they know. Your job is to help them to see if their 'new' ideas stand up. That is the beginning of an intellectual life.

Here it is crucial that the teacher does not appear bored by what might well seem perceptions of the obvious. After all, what may be old hat to you or to the learned world may be revelations or earth-shattering or wonderful glimpses to a pupil. Your pupils, each year, are new. Keep the excitement in the air. Ask a lot of them, but don't ask too much. Let them sometimes see and feel the full force of your mind, to sense that you really do have a fair bit in your back pocket, but that should take second place to establishing an atmosphere in which they can intellectually breathe and exercise and grow.

One word of warning. There is a certain kind of dominating, greedy teacher, greedy to impress his head, greedy for success, and (worst of all) greedy for every minute his pupils may have. Each pupil is made to feel that only *this teacher's* subject matters, that work must be always done first in this subject, and everything else comes equal bottom of the list. If this teacher's examination results are better than any other department's, as unsurprisingly they may well be, the problem can become deep-seated.

We are here faced with another manifestation of the guru problem. This is closer to indoctrination than expectation. It can kill off pupils: once they have seen through the unreal demands such a teacher is making they often turn strongly against the subject.

By their very insistence on winning, such teachers lose.

OK, we must be at least halfway through the lesson now, and

you've been very patient, so I'm going to tell you a story. All you have to do is sit back and listen, and anyone who doesn't want to listen can leave now.

All right?

David Smith, come back here!

23
The Teacher And The Judge

There was a teacher – this, by the way, for those who like to know, is a true story – and he was an inspiring teacher who loved his pupils and said unusual things and uncovered unusual talents in the young, talents they did not even know they had. He taught them not only to love books and ideas but he went on walks with them and taught them to listen to the call of birds, to look closely into rivers and to feel the spirit of the woods. I know this because he was a friend of mine. No one could doubt that he made his pupils want to learn and that he made the world a better place.

But he led an unconventional life.

Anyway, one day – a hot day – this teacher, my friend, found himself sitting in court and being accused, rightly, of adultery. His third marriage was on the rocks and this was in those distant days when divorces required a guilty party, and a guilty party he knew he was.

The judge on the case took it upon himself, however, to deliver some harsh criticisms, some unnecessarily harsh criticisms, of the teacher's private life. These criticisms not only made his private life public but also the institution where he worked was named, because the judge's comments were picked up by the quality papers who were even then beginning to compete with the popular press for their share of the tittle-tattle. Although well aware of his own weaknesses with women, the teacher was not amused the next day to open his quality paper and to read what he had already heard the judge say to his face in that very hot courtroom.

The teacher, a most sensitive man, thought the judge had gone too far, far too far, so he contacted those few of his friends who were in high places – not me, of course – those friends, I mean, who lived amongst the Great and the Good. He contacted them quickly, one by one, and asked them if they knew this judge or happened to know of this judge. Such is the network in this country that three of his contacts did know of the judge, two of them knew him a little and one in particular knew the judge very well indeed.

And here the teacher had his first moment of luck. The one who knew the judge very well indeed did not like him one little bit and told the teacher that the judge had not only been a pompous and self-satisfied ass at university but had grown into an even more pompous and self-satisfied ass during his years on the bench.

As if that was not enough, on further detailed enquiry and with the help of wheels within wheels, it seemed that the judge, when he was away from home and supposedly being judicial elsewhere, was not above meeting a woman (not his wife) in a rented cottage in a particularly lovely area on the South Downs and in sight and sound of the sea. To use the language of those times, the judge – it seemed – had a popsie.

Because in such delicate matters he liked to be absolutely sure of his facts, my friend the teacher checked out this morsel of information: he hated any feeling of unwarranted animosity and it was no part of his code to intrude on other people's lives. He was not a vindictive man. Even so, he visited the small village on the South Downs, travelling down in his

Austin Mini Countryman (for he was a countryman at heart), calling in at the pub, the village store and the post office. It was a lovely spot, the sort of village – as P. G. Wodehouse put it – where picturesque cottages breed like rabbits.

This was in the summer holidays, the long summer holidays (for teachers have long summer holidays, a fact of which they are often reminded and over which they are supposedly meant to feel a lifetime of guilt, as if holidays without any money to spend are a form of handsome reimbursement), and in his long summer holiday, with time on his hands and a copy of Wordsworth's *The Prelude* (the 1805 edition) in his pocket, the teacher stayed at a homely bed and breakfast and made some friends in the pub. Soon he was familiar with the locals, he played dominoes and shove-ha'penny and darts, and this led him, as such things do, to meet the lady who cleaned at the house at which the judge – or so it was alleged – periodically entertained his popsie.

By friendly talk and a little bribery the teacher even found out that the judge always discreetly contacted the cleaning lady to inform her when he was next due to come down, and the cleaning lady told the teacher this fact because she had never liked the way the judge talked to her. He did not, she said, talk to her as a gentleman should. By contrast she did like the way the teacher talked to her, and she also liked the twenty pounds the teacher handed her. Twenty pounds was a lot of money in those days.

Each day the teacher looked at the judge's empty cottage. Hard though he tried not to feel the emotion he couldn't help looking at it enviously, it was such a pretty place, and though only a second or rented home it was much nicer than any home the teacher himself would ever own. It really was the most perfect hideaway, a paradise for an overworked judge who needed to get away from it all and relax. Each day the teacher also got to know the area surrounding the cottage and

the garden a little better, looking at it from all angles, sometimes risking going in by the front latch gate and then by the
back gate, a gate which led on, as luck would have it, to
Lovers' Lane, though the name was almost covered up with
tall nettles and cow parsley.

Something suddenly caught his eye.

From the front gate, the teacher walked stealthily, carefully,
counting deliberately to himself and occasionally looking over
his shoulder, as one might pace out a cricket pitch (twenty-two
yards), until he came to a small copse across the road. Here, in
this copse, he found a bower as hidden, as virginal as the one
the young Wordsworth found when 'Nutting', the bower he
suddenly and pointlessly raped. This bower was thirty-one
yards, give or take a foot, from the front gate.

It was a beauteous evening, calm and free, as the teacher
first crouched, then lay in the grass, eyeing the gate. He felt
his heart. He stood up, repaced the distance, and found it was
still thirty-one yards, give or take a foot. He went back to the
pub: he needed to think, he needed a drink.

By a further bribe the very next day, the teacher (whose
charm with women in the first place had led him to this village on the South Downs) encouraged the cleaning lady to
telephone him with news of the judge's next arrival: for a further twenty pounds, which was much more than the judge
ever paid her for her cleaning and discretion, she agreed to do
this. Indeed, in her heart of hearts, she would have done it for
nothing.

The teacher now left his bed and breakfast and drove back
to his modest home and every evening, as dusk fell, he would
walk out into the local park, put his jacket down, move away
thirty-one paces and lie down. He knew he could do it, but to
keep his mind as sharp and as in focus as it needed to be, he
foreswore all relations with women and all alcohol until this
matter was resolved to his satisfaction.

One morning the telephone rang. After toast and honey and one cup of strong coffee he drove his Austin Mini Countryman back to the small village and parked it as close as he could to the copse. He looked at the house and circled the property to make quite sure no one was in and to make quite sure everything was as he remembered it, and then walked very naturally to the front garden gate. Taking from his pocket a long piece of very fine wire, he wound this round and round the latch. The wire was so fine you had to look hard to see it.

After checking that the gate would not open he retired to his car by the copse. He sat waiting, with his field glasses already out of their case. To pass the time he focused on a lesser spotted woodpecker – such a shy, elusive bird, with a soft ringing call – some gilded butterflies and the extraordinary cloud formations high above him. What skies there had been that month! His mind ran over that verse in 'Adlestrop':

> And willows, willow-herb, and grass,
> And meadowsweet, and haycocks dry,
> No whit less still and lonely fair
> Than the high cloudlets in the sky.

The memory of the poem made him feel more at peace with himself.

Just over an hour later a man and a woman arrived at the front gate. The teacher knew it was the judge. Magnified by the field glasses, the judge (even without his wig) looked all too familiar and all too close. That the woman was not his wife was only too obvious from his ingratiating attentiveness – the adulterer stood courteously aside to allow his popsie to go first through the gate. The teacher opened the boot of his car.

But the gate would not budge; her little hand could only rattle it. The teacher smiled and nodded to himself: work on, my medicine, work. The judge asked her to step aside. The teacher was now lying on the grass, but he was not laughing. The judge, a little annoyed at this strange business, some village louts no doubt, what's the country coming to, leant over the gate to undo the offending fine wire: oh, honestly, whoever had been fooling around had made a good job of it. His popsie told him it was silly to get annoyed, it was nothing.

Even in the fading light, the judge – as he bent over the garden gate – presented a clear, broad picture to a keenly trained pair of eyes. The teacher, a sportsman, a countryman, a passionate lover of Wordsworth and of women and of the world of teaching, looked steadily through his sights at the broad backside of the judge, aimed, squeezed and fired. The noise startled all the birds in the bower as he peppered those broad buttocks with both barrels.

The teacher stood and calmly packed his gun away, making not the slightest effort to conceal himself, and drove slowly off through the village. As the village fell away behind him he lowered his window and breathed in deeply the country air. What a glorious evening it was! It made you glad to be alive.

The judge, for his part, did not for a while take his seat on the bench. Nor was this incident ever reported to the police, or recorded in any of the papers.

24
The Importance Of
Double Standards

Judges who judge teachers.
Teachers who teach judges.
Which brings me nicely to double standards.

Teachers can, we all agree, inspire you for life. Teachers can, it
is often said, ruin your life. Teachers stand for much that is
good in our society. Teachers, especially the bad gurus, often
have a dark, dangerous streak. There was a recent studio discussion on television – I watched it in my dentist's waiting
room – and those taking part, all very successful adults, were
equally divided between the ones who had been set on their
path in life by the shaping influence of a very special teacher
and those who had been so damned and discouraged at school
that they made it their long-term aim to 'prove those small-
minded bastards wrong'. In my anecdotal experience the
second group is the larger, with more people claiming they suffered lasting damage than reaffirming their eternal gratitude.

With my mouth anaesthetised and my teeth being drilled,
I felt yet again the full weight of this divide. It has long bothered me. Are we teachers really such a force for good and/or
ill?

If so, it's awesome. If so, we are the central profession.

If we can make or break any child, the country at large should be hanging on our every word and asking our advice on every issue. But I don't sense it is. And if I bounced out of bed each day, fully aware of my capacity to lead them all to the promised land or to cause large-scale damage, I would not last very long. Indeed, what with my halo and my baggage, I doubt I would even get out of bed: I'd never get over myself.

This takes us deep into the question of moral authority and guidance, of the higher expectation, because in this country a teacher's role and influence is clearly seen as a much wider one than simply teaching his academic subject and preparing his pupils for public examinations. If we are in danger of being looked up to, the question mark over our worthiness begins to glow.

A close friend, for some years a successful teacher before he left the profession, has often told me he found it increasingly difficult to tell any pupils off because he 'had done everything himself'. With his record of misconduct ever before his eyes he just could not stand up there saying things he did not believe. As he opened his mouth to remonstrate with a pupil or a class, he saw his past life flashing before him, his casual sex, his drinking, his drugs, his petty cruelties, his dishonesties, all the many actions large and small he would rather have shredded into the bin but which his conscience preferred to print out before his eyes in bold capitals. He felt a hypocrite. And being a hypocrite is exactly the charge most often thrown by the young at their parents and at their teachers. 'You're a hypocrite' hurts, especially when – as your profession often requires – you are trying to take a stand on something. 'You're a hypocrite' sticks, especially when you are also saying it daily to yourself.

Indeed, people ask me if I struggle not only with the professional demands in the classroom but also the wider social constraints of being a teacher. Teachers (a bit like vicars) are obliged and expected and meant to behave well, to behave rather better than others, to set an example – arguably, with the ever-declining influence of the churches, teachers feel this even more so. If a teacher misbehaves in a major way, which usually means minor sex, the press love it. Teacher does this, teacher does that. Suddenly the press are all crowded together on the upper reaches of the Matterhorn, waving their flags on the high moral ground. What chance has our country got when our teachers, who should know better, who should be setting us an example, behave like that? Would you want your kid sitting in a class taught by this bloke? *Quis custodiet ipsos custodes?* The question Juvenal shrewdly put in his *Satires* still bites hard today: how can we have confidence in the people in positions of trust if they abuse it?

If, of course, you rise to the top of your profession and become a head, not only is that the end of your private life (too busy), but you'll need to be a beacon of goodness in public. Difficult to let your hair down. Difficult, for example, to get pissed with your mates. Difficult if you fall for someone. And if you secretly plan to do whatever naughty thing you want to do well away from your home area or usual stamping grounds, the first person you'll encounter is a pupil or parent. The eyes of a disapproving world are trained on you, waiting for you to fall. All you need is someone to blow the whistle.

When the head of a major public school 'fell from grace' a few years ago, he said that one of his greatest reliefs was that he didn't have to pretend any more; at long last, I suppose, he could be himself and leave the Matterhorn to those who wanted to stand on it. No more pulpits, no more the daily call to be censorious, no more pupils assessing you. Nothing more to lose. He was fed up with walking the tight-rope, of trying to be someone more impressive than he was. Now that he was known he could get on with the rest of his life. I can see the appeal in all that. I have felt it.

This tension – between the public figure you cut (your image of how you wish the world to see you) and how you really are – has long been a preoccupation of mine. For my profession it is a supremely uncomfortable moral dilemma, and I explored it in *The Head Man*, the series of eight plays I wrote for BBC radio. That series was partly drawn from my own unresolved nature and from observing my colleagues but mainly triggered by having to listen (before I dropped the habit and found happiness) to headmasters preaching from the pulpit. For too long I had watched them politicking all the way from their study into the vestry before the service, and all the way back from the vestry to their study after the service, and I wondered what on earth was going on in their hearts and minds in the service and, most particularly, when they were up in the pulpit preaching. But, then again, if you had to be pure to preach I suppose there would be a lot fewer sermons. (Hang on, that's rather a good idea. I'm beginning to think only the pure should preach.)

But no. The truth is you have to tell lies. You have to be a hypocrite. It goes with the territory. You have to be shocked when you're not. You have to embrace double standards. You have to promote what you do not believe. And the trick, of course, is to know that you are doing it. You must not believe your own propaganda. If you do that, you're lost. You have to hold up a model approach knowing full well you do not yourself embody it. You do this because the model approach, the religious or moral or intellectual example you are offering to the young, is a much better one than your own life. You can't in all seriousness start saying to your pupils or to your own children, 'Hey, look at the hypocritical mess I am, why don't you model yourself on *that*?'

When I am in the staff common room and colleagues are

working themselves into a regular lather about some piece of misconduct, coming on strong about how absolutely appalled they are by this or how shocked they are by that, I can never tell whether they really are as morally rocked as they say. Still, don't let's give them a post-modernist shrug; let's give them the benefit of the doubt. Let us say they are as shocked as they appear. Well, if they are, they're much better than I am. If they're not, they're pretty average hypocrites like the rest of us, and I wish they'd air their burgeoning professional outrage only in front of the young. At least there it might do some good.

In so far, however, as you do offer a model, a teacher or parent should do so without straining the moral contrasts, without implying that he himself exemplifies these virtues while the pupil or child does not; and 'always avoiding', in A. C. Benson's words, 'the subtle temptation to speak more impressively than he feels in the cause of right'.

Indeed no one better embodies the problem of double standards than A. C. Benson himself, whose words flow like a tributary through this book, because he knew and described this public–private turmoil. Though the phrase post-dates his life, he instinctively lived double standards, and it therefore comes as no surprise that he wrote one of the very best books about the world of teaching. It is also no surprise that he received anonymous obscene letters when it was published. Every day – at Eton, at Windsor Castle, at Cambridge, at Lambeth – he walked the corridors of power, arm in arm (sometimes literally) with the Great and the Good, conducting a dignified establishment life which demanded a high moral tone. He operated the system. Many teachers, uncomfortable though it may leave them, find it best to do the same. As Evelyn Waugh puts it so memorably in *Decline and Fall*, 'we schoolmasters must temper discretion with deceit'.

In public it was all cathedral closes for Benson, all courts

and cloisters, castles and private pews. Deference and cere-
mony and double standards. His father, E. W. Benson, had
been Wellington College's first headmaster, before going on to
become the Bishop of Truro and, eventually, a most zealous
Archbishop of Canterbury. A. C. Benson did not exactly
follow in his father's footsteps, but he chose a similarly
approved path. He became a housemaster at Eton, before
going on to become Master of Magdalene College,
Cambridge: 'the superior, well-endowed, leisurely don,' as he
himself sharply put it, 'who despises the rough and tumble of
the world and lives in elegant seclusion'. Beyond the classroom and the college he was always welcome at Windsor
where he found time to edit Queen Victoria's letters. After
dining with her in December 1899 he wrote in his diary, 'No
doubt it was the first time that a schoolmaster pure and
simple – not a headmaster or clergyman – had ever sat at that
table.' As well as being a conventional figure of consequence,
indeed one of The Elect, he also published many successful
books. And – a rather curious footnote, this – after collabo-
rating with Elgar, he wrote the words of 'Land of Hope and
Glory'. Now, I bet not many people know that.

It was not, of course, at all like that underneath. It rarely is.
Far from being 'a schoolmaster pure and simple' and later 'a
leisurely don', he was as much cursed as blessed. Beneath the
Pomp and Circumstance his family was strange and tragic,
with a thread of despair if not insanity running through it.
He himself suffered great emotional insecurity and self-
repression; 'like a figure at the end of the avenue', he felt an
unsatisfied hunger for affection, yet he remained frightened of
love – indeed, he was too cautious and too timid even to
reach out for it. A suitable case, if ever there was one, for
Anthony Storr's therapy.

Yet although he was crippled by depression he was an outstanding housemaster. With his effortless ease of speech he

taught brilliantly in the classroom, and he later became a great benefactor of Magdalene College. His friendships with the young men he taught, though no doubt full of temptation, were 'like flying sunlight on a bright morning'. As for his private thoughts, he preferred to pour those, all five million secret words, into 180 volumes of diaries. There he wrote pen pictures of the leading figures in late Victorian and Edwardian England: shrewd, perceptive, edgy, gripping observations, detailing the longings, doubts and hatreds of a bitchily self-obsessed man trying to get 'some of the venom out of my system'.

When I think of the lessons to be learnt over hypocrisy and double standards, my mind clicks to Benson. Putting it another way (and at the risk of a preachy tone), I would say remember what you have done, know your temptations, remember who you are, who you really are – at your open best and at your secret worst – and let that inform your understanding and your treatment of the young in your care.

25
The Value Of Not Being Yourself

'Be Yourself', I advised earlier.

Well, I'm afraid that won't quite do. It's time to move from the mask of hypocrisy to the heart of drama. It's time to talk about acting and sport.

The single experience I most enjoyed as a schoolboy was acting the part of Sir Andrew Aguecheek in *Twelfth Night*. Every night I was racing with expectation and high with happiness. Oh, yes, 'I delight in masks and revels sometimes altogether.' The most fun I had in my first job – at Loretto, an all-boys school – was dressing up as a gawky, goshy woman and playing the role of the gym mistress, Miss Gossage, in a staff production of *The Happiest Days of Your Life*. Oh, yes, 'I'm Miss Gossage, call me sausage.' (Eat your heart out, Joyce Grenfell.) The moments which keep coming back to me, the achievements of which I am most proud in my career as a teacher, particularly in my years at Tonbridge, are not the examination results or the sporting triumphs but some of the plays I have directed. Indeed, acting is very much on my mind at the moment as I am about to direct another play, and this one's probably my last.

Furthermore, over the last twenty years, since I started to

write radio and television drama, I have worked with many first-rate actors, names big and small, and watched them bring to life the parts I wrote. There is something about the company of professional actors, the stories they tell, the voices and accents they can do, which appeals to me as a teacher as much as a writer. I admire their timing and skill, and I watch the way their timing and skill holds attention. They make me laugh, they make me cry, they make me wait. Although timing is partly God-given, from actors I have learnt the value and potential power of a pause, the slight withholding of a response, which can be moving or funny or devastating. In the classroom and in social life this can be as effective as on stage.

When actors talk of their own schooldays they can improvise and imitate a whole world of teachers and pupils before my eyes. They catch the imperative gestures, the magisterial tones of voice, the shakily undermined authority, the craven look of panic in a teacher's eye. (Even better, when actors say of my script, during a lunch break or afterwards in the pub, 'It's so easy, it just comes off the page,' I feel tremendous pleasure and gratitude. All those hours of working on the dialogue, of trying to catch it just right, all the ups and downs of a creative life, have paid off. And, as it's the world of acting, and I'm now a writer not a teacher, I can hug them.)

Acting and teaching are, in some ways, very similar. Actors and teachers, both professions have to perform. So do parents. Actors and teachers have to turn up on time, look and sound the part, pump the adrenalin and do it. To be late for your entry or late on cue for an actor is unforgivable and probably fatal for the scene, if not for the whole production. Teachers too often get away with being late. Actors and teachers have nerves – I feel sick with apprehension in the wings before each term – because when teachers go into class or actors go on stage they know all eyes will be on them. Or should be on them. To be good, which means have the ability to ensure such attention, actors need stage presence (The Look). They must know how to stand in an authoritative way (don't shuffle or move your feet!), how to play higher or lower status, when to take centre stage and how to fade (Coming Second).

One professional actress (does one say 'actor' or 'actress'?) I saw playing Lady Macbeth certainly had the potential to be a great teacher. It was during a matinée in the West End, which was being ruined by the obligatory rows of schoolchildren eating and talking nonstop throughout the performance. In the middle of the banquet scene she suddenly stood up, left her husband to his nervous breakdown, walked to the front of the stage, pointed at the offending rows in the auditorium and said, 'Shut The Fuck Up!' Terrific. I cheered. I stamped. (Silently, of course, because when I once remonstrated with another such talking group behind me – not from my own school – they sprayed the back of my jacket with ink and chewing gum.) Still, as for that Lady Macbeth, she was welcome in our staff room any time. When things got tough on the discipline front she wouldn't mind a bit of blood on her hands.

The actor has to interact and work with the other actors on stage, as well as know how to communicate with the audience. He has to be heard – to pitch and project – and to be seen. For a performer in the theatre or in the classroom or in the sporting arena, there is no hiding place. The story he tells, and the role he plays, must be convincing. If he overacts he needs to be corrected, because overacting or mannered acting means that everyone can see you are acting, whereas the whole point about good acting is that no one thinks you are acting. The trick is that you are acting but you're acting so well it all looks natural. Far from being natural, of course, it is an art, the art that hides art. For his part, the teacher has to woo his audience and to win them into a listening and learning mood.

The actor has a script, which he has to learn by heart. He

must know his stuff. The teacher may have a lesson plan, an outline scenario of how he wants the next forty minutes to go, but he has no agreed script. To help himself through his daily performance the teacher has, over the years, probably stocked his head with a variety of well-worn tapes which, when tired or under pressure, he can put on. Perhaps all too often he may be tempted to press one of these Play buttons and switch himself off. And run on auto. Which is bad. We've all done it, obviously, and we all do it, but it is still bad. Once you switch off and allow routine reactions and predictable responses to take over, your pupils notice. They quickly pick up non-listening teachers; they can read your eyes just as easily as you read theirs.

One hot afternoon one of my friends went further than switching off and pulling out the plug; he actually fell asleep while teaching. When he came to the surface he could hear himself still talking on auto and he could see his pupils were still taking notes. He was pleased to find that what he heard coming out of his mouth sounded rather good stuff.

While performing on stage or in the classroom, you are both yourself and not yourself. Or, rather, more than yourself and not quite yourself. Your real self informs your acting self. Your selves talk to each other. At your best what is coming out of your mouth is being skilfully monitored and edited by what is going on in your head. Some actors can only act one part, and they end up acting that act. They may often become very successful at it and establish their profile with that performance. With that success, of course, comes the danger that they may become caricatures of themselves, or rather of the roles they have created for themselves. The same fate can befall teachers: they become locked into a professional role they have written, e.g. the world-weary cynic, or the long-suffering saint, or the bright and breezy song-and-dance man, or the reliable robot. They then take this, and only this, into class with them.

Just as by using a semi-fictional narrator, or persona, the novelist may hope to throw off the scent those critics who wish to draw impertinently close biographical parallels between his fiction and his real life, so the teacher may choose to play a part in class which is a mixture of his natural self and his performing self. He is, as it were, in the public domain but wishes and needs a part of himself to remain hidden. Like a Japanese or Elizabethan actor he has put on a mask more colourful than his own face. It may be a purely theatrical mask or a psychologically protective face or a bit of both. While this can make a teacher's nature somewhat elusive or lay him open to the charge that he is finally unknowable, that may be a price he is willing or indeed has to pay. If he feels too exposed and too vulnerable, if he is prone to take everything to heart, it may all become too much. He may need somewhere to run and to hide.

One of the joys of teaching is that you can try your hand at so many things: be a jack of all trades and master of some. Before I leave the question of acting teachers and teaching actors, however, I want (at the risk of writing a bit of narrative) to describe what it is like to produce a school play. I want to do this because it is the experience which has most often fulfilled or stretched or, in the current jargon, challenged me. One of the best ways to learn in any field – be it academic, artistic or sporting – is to imitate, to try on an idea for size, to find if something fits you, to dress oneself in a pattern of thoughts, to watch others who perform better than you, to be part of a team and yet to stand alone and accept that there is no hiding place. On both a practical and a metaphoric level, school drama offers the perfect teaching model for this.

A play is a consuming commitment. The time, effort and discipline demanded from each member of the cast, and from the whole production team, is so intense that I have never been able to string more than three productions together before stepping aside to rebuild my strength and morale. I sense that if I do one more production I could be finished. That way madness lies.

It can also feel uphill all the way for the producer because in many schools more time, more status and more allowance is made for sport and for music than for drama. Furthermore, there still lurks among many teachers and heads an unspoken puritan suspicion of acting, of dressing up, of the psycho-emotional, of the whole business of becoming someone else. It's the same with dancing. Playing in an orchestra, however, is fine. There the pupil sits, properly dressed, with his violin or trumpet. Nothing dodgy about that, all above board and under the baton. Playing outdoor games is OK too, that's healthy. So, sport and music are safe. But who can tell what those dodgy actors might not get up to?

The production, from choosing the text to the final night, can dominate a teacher's every waking moment for up to three months, not to mention interrupt his sleep pattern. Selecting the play in the first place is such a difficult decision: do we have the right actors, will the school like it, is it too difficult, will they be up to speaking verse or should we settle for prose, are we going for easy success rather than a demanding experience, can we get away with it, big cast or small, classical or modern, English or foreign, shall we do a musical (leave your brain in the foyer) or a difficult new play? . . . Right, let's go for it.

Then the auditions. Agonies of indecision, moving the parts around, trying to get the chemistry right, trying to be fair, trying not to hurt. If I get it wrong now it'll never be right, it'll be like appointing a bad colleague or marrying the wrong person. Do I give that part to a totally reliable pupil who, like a spaniel at my heels, is desperate to be involved or to the unreliable-but-gifted one who'll cut some rehearsals? On the other hand, if the unreliable-but-gifted one accepts the discipline it's a big step forward for him, and partly that's what I'm in education for. Here the artistic director and the social worker clash.

Next, organise rehearsal schedules, four or five rehearsals a week, plus some weekends. Book rooms, spaces, design the set, costumes, tickets, programme, deal with likely clashes (these are likely to be in sport and music, because performers tend to perform in many areas) and conflicting loyalties. Can I risk the rehearsals going pear-shaped because some actor is playing the piccolo? And what about sport? Do I want a Romeo with a broken leg or a stamped-on face? Are his games an acceptable risk? Is it fair on the rest of the cast? Equally, he might be told by his games coach that if he takes on that part in the play and is not available for every training session he won't get picked for any matches. That isn't fair either. (I am not looking forward to these professional disputes.)

Throughout the term you rehearse each line, each speech, every movement, work on changing the pace, work on memory, on voice, on how to move and how to stand, how to use the stage and how to use your eyes, to control your hands and feet, to keep your head up, to be courageous, to be clear, to be subtle, to be patient, to touch each other, to act natural, to take criticism, to have fun, to do it again and again and again . . . to earn your success and the audience's applause. You want them to applaud at the end, don't you? Well, earn it! Why should anyone applaud you if you're not up to it?

Above all I want to instil in them the value of team work. Never is there a greater chance for self-expression than in drama and never a greater need for self-discipline. For unbounded energy within a sense of wholeness. While acting and drama does for some people what psychoanalysis does for others (releases, gives expression to the unconscious, and confronts), it also insists upon the actor understanding his social function. To put that less grandly: if one actor, however minor, fails to come on or gets up himself or tarts it up or starts looking at the audience, the whole damn thing is ruined. If the play is to take off we need poise, we need collective self-expression, and all that must be held within a disciplined framework.

And what is the producer thinking? Keep going, keep battling through the down patches, you never should have cast that arrogant sod, no, he's better today, give him the benefit of the doubt, it's beginning to come, no it isn't, we're miles off, why is it so hard to get there, ease off on this actor, put pressure on that one now, can he take the strain, she's terrific, she always is, do we need music here, who'll write the music, he said he'd write the music, why doesn't that scene work, she's funny, when she looks at him he can't go on, no, it's good, keep going, sometimes there's magic in the air.

It is extraordinary and sometimes unreasonable to see the level of skill you demand and the mixture of energy and vulnerability you take for granted. You try to feel concern for everyone's sensitivity but you need to be tough enough to take control of the whole group and shake it, demand more, insist on more, without losing their goodwill and without losing the sense of creative fun which gives the production its humanity.

By the opening night you know almost everything about the strengths and weaknesses of the cast. As they do of you. They see the teacher stripped of his classroom act and style, they sometimes hear effing and blinding. Some of the most unprofessional things I have threatened, or screamed, have been in school productions and usually at those selfless technicians in charge of sound. The more brilliantly computerised the sound system becomes, the more they tell you it can't go wrong, the bigger the chance of a colossal balls-up. Don't ask me why, just go along to the dress rehearsal and listen. The main sound you hear is the heavy hum of the speakers with no other effects.

Start on time, every line is right, they're doing it, loud and clear, and it's moving along at a cracking pace, timing's good, it's really happening, you risk a thumbs-up, every lighting cue bang on, that was a nice scene change, and the first sound cue . . . WHAT! . . . I'll kill him, I will, with my bare hands, I'm going up there now, I've f——— warned him, I'll chuck him over the balcony, he can't say he wasn't warned, watch the body coming over . . .

But on the first night, they do it. Actors *and* technicians.

> *We've done it!*
> *I had a novel on TV!*
> *We had crossed the Alps!*

Punch the air. Hug everyone? (No, better not. Children's Act.) When I was younger, stupidly, I used to walk away from it all afterwards, as if it was nothing to do with me, and did not properly celebrate. I regret that now. I see it as a form of mock-modesty, a form of conceit, or at least a refusal to accept thanks. Now I like to see their wild-eyed faces, wild at what they have achieved. By not being themselves, by becoming someone else, they have found new limits, they have found out more about life and what it feels to be other people: they have learnt and grown. They deserve the applause. I apologise to the sound people and feel enormous affection and respect for everyone – individually and collectively – for what they have given.

What has it all been? In a word, education.

26
The Point

A lead-pencil has a point, an argument may have a point, remarks may be pointed, and a man who wants to borrow five pounds from you only comes to the point when he asks you for the fiver. Lots of things have points: especially weapons. But where is the point to life? Where is the point to love? Where, if it comes to the point, is the point to a bunch of violets? There is no point. Life and love are life and love, a bunch of violets is a bunch of violets, and to drag in the idea of a point is to ruin everything. Live and let live, love and let love, flower and fade, and follow the natural curve, which flows on, pointless.

D. H. LAWRENCE (1885–1930)

27

The Place For Games

– So, you went to school in Wales?

– That's right, Christ College, Brecon.

– That's a rugby school, isn't it?

– They play rugby pretty well, yes. But I wouldn't—

– And you first taught . . . somewhere in . . . Scotland,
wasn't it?

– Yes, at Loretto School, in Musselburgh, just south of
Edinburgh—

– That's a rugby school, isn't it?

– Yes, they play rugby pretty well too, but I wouldn't
say—

– But most of your career you've been at Tonbridge?

– I have, well over thirty years now. Hard to believe,
isn't—

– So you must like it? Tonbridge?

– I do, yes, I like it a lot.

– Cricket school, isn't it?

– The school does play cricket, yes, they – we – play it
pretty well, but—

– Colin Cowdrey went there, didn't he?

– That's right. And so did E. M. Forster, and Freddie

Forsyth, as well as Patrick Mayhew, and Christopher
Reid, and Vikram Seth—
– Vikram Seth?
– I told you that before. Concentrate!
– Sorry.
– Though only in the sixth form – and Vikram Jayanti,
the film producer. In fact quite a few of the poems I've
got on my classroom walls were written by Tonbridgians.
Sidney Keyes, of course, who was killed in the Second
World War. Keyes, Reid, Seth, I'm proud of them all.
And E. M. Forster, though he's not a poet. It's not a
matter, I hope, of appropriating them, but I'm a bit of a
hero-worshipper, and I enjoy the feeling that I'm walking
around and working where they did – we're back to how
Wordsworth felt about Milton at Cambridge, and how I
felt about going to the same college as Wordsworth. And,
of course, this is especially true of E. M. Forster.
– But he wasn't particularly happy at Tonbridge, was he?
– Not particularly.
– And that doesn't bother you?
– It isn't all that important either way. I suspect most
interesting, creative people weren't very happy at school,
and I suspect that will continue to be the case. I am more
concerned with what people *do* with their lives. I don't
look at my pupils and think, 'Are they happy?' Perhaps I
should, but I don't. I think, 'Are they interested?' I'll
settle for that. Being interested means so much.
Sometimes I'm a bit worried that if we make being at
school nicer and nicer, which I think we are, we'll end up
without any writers.
– You're not serious?
– Partly.
– They must say something about you, then, these poems?
– Perhaps they do, they're mostly from that part of the

English tradition that means the most to me, the deep
line that runs from Wordsworth to Hardy to Edward
Thomas to Larkin. All that speaks to me, I can't imagine
a day without them in my mind, I'm always seeing them
and hearing them. It's like that moment in Westminster
Abbey, at Ted Hughes's memorial service, when you
heard his recorded voice, you unexpectedly heard his
voice again, from beyond the grave, and you thought, no,
that's right, he's still with us, he always will be.

– You feel it *that* personally?

– I can't exaggerate it. It's a presence, a kind of music. It's
all around me and in me. I like to be reminded, each day,
of all my influences. In the same way I would miss my
Wordsworth poster, I love my photos of Chet Baker and
Ben Webster, and of Philip Larkin looking hilariously
grumpy, and Betjeman beside himself laughing, and the
ones of Christopher Isherwood and Edward Thomas.

– Is Edward Thomas particularly important?

– Well, I named my son after him. His poetry makes
me . . . attend . . . and listen and look more closely at the
world. At the simple, enduring things. Take 'Adlestrop',
it's such a simple piece, apparently, yet it grows and grows
as you think about it, which is what art should do . . .
That poem has influenced a huge amount of poetry since,
and that pleases me. A lot of show-off art diminishes the
more you look at it . . . Edward Thomas has always been a
model for me and for many writers. 'Anything,' he said,
'however small, may make a work of art; concentrating
intensity of mood is the only necessary condition.'

– What else do you have on your walls?

– Well, the Augustus John painting of Dylan Thomas,
which my father gave me. Edward Thomas and Dylan
Thomas remind me of my Anglo-Welsh roots. I feel
they're up there keeping an eye on me, to make sure I

don't become too Kentish.
– Talking of Kent, did all the Cowdreys go to Tonbridge, then?
– Sorry? Oh, yes, all the sons, yes. Not the daughter, of course.
– Oh, single sex, is it?
– Yes.
– Your son plays cricket, doesn't he?
– Yes, he's a professional. He likes it.
– At Tonbridge, was he?

In a certain kind of English-middle-class-one-upmanship-social-chat there is a cheaply competitive way of putting down sport, particularly competitive sport, and most particularly competitive sport in schools. Propping up that kind of talk, and bolstering the self-esteem of those who indulge in it, is the assumption that if you have a mind, if you read books and play music, if you see yourself as any kind of an intellectual, you cannot possibly take sport seriously. To take sport seriously would be too sad. Forget *mens sana in corpore sano*. Anyone with a brain, the assumption goes, spends his schooldays trying to get out of any form of games. Possibly a gentle game of pat-ball tennis, (especially if it's for a laugh), or a jog, or a long country walk, or a bit of ski-ing, that's all right, but the general line-up is:

> the intellectual v. the rugger-bugger
> the aesthete v. the athlete
> the arty v. the jock-strap
> the mind v. the balls
> the cerebral v. the hearty
> the enlightened v. the philistines

The put-down-sport picture is one of overdeveloped bodies

and underdeveloped minds, of caring more about who's in the team than academic work, of yobbish students singing dirty songs in the back of the bus, of rugby players smashing up hotels, muddied oafs vomiting all over the carpet, and a general licence for the kind of graceless behaviour both on and off the field of play which is more rightly called violent and should have you arrested and charged with GBH. (And some of that unpleasant caricature rings true. I've been there, seen it, done it. And I dislike it all very much.)

For the vast majority of pupils, however, who love exercise and enjoy playing games (not computer games, but open-air team games, competitive games), that is a caricature. Worse still, in many schools the pass on sport has increasingly been sold. So, sadly, has the land on which the school games were once played. Millions of pupils now miss out. The national picture is patchy, county by county, but far too few maintained schools organise competitive games well, if at all. Millions of pupils, who would enjoy nothing more than representing their school in football or cricket or in any number of games, simply never have that chance.

Some of this can be laid at the door of the egalitarian notion that competitive sport is bad. It's bad because someone has to lose, and we can't have that because it's unkind, isn't it, children, it really isn't very nice to be a loser, so we won't play at all, so there! Yet playing for the school – win, lose or draw – is a thrill which adult sport is unlikely to equal. Why should children not have that physical and mental challenge, and that physical and mental pleasure, and learn to deal with winning and losing, learn to win graciously and to lose graciously – and find out how difficult all that is? But, difficult or not, it should be an essential part of education. When you have lost, saying 'thank you' (through gritted teeth while biting your lip) to some opposition players – let alone the referee – is acting of the highest order. As well as being tough, as well as being fun, it is another way of learning about yourself.

It does not end there. The ironies are even worse. Those who are lucky enough to have school sport laid on, who do play or shine, be it in the maintained or the independent sector, must tippex it out of their profiles. Given the current orthodoxy, when filling in their UCAS forms or Oxbridge application forms, boys and girls would be well advised not to mention their record or expertise in sport. More than likely, a sporting CV will work against you:

'Ugh, you play games!'

'A rugger-bugger!'

(Camp shudder.)

The idea or the goal of the all-rounder is derided. To be an intellectual in sport is a no-no (unless you're a French or Italian football manager). To be a sportsman in intellectual circles is a no-no. 'He's too clever to be a good sportsman.' Or 'He's too keen on games to be much of an intellectual.' The Renaissance hero, the C. B. Fry figure (a great all-round athlete, scholar and arresting conversationalist), is dead, a turn-off, lbw, as out of date as the figures on the frieze of the Parthenon, comic even, eliciting a smugly specialist smile, kicked into touch and mocked by a set of liberal attitudes every bit as unpleasant as some of the ugly prejudices to be found amongst sports fanatics.

All this is very curious, as it sits uneasily with the across-the-board quasi-religious cult of New Football. For the last ten years, while the anti-competitive games lobby in schools has grown and provision for school sport has declined, professional football has become gentrified. Everyone – of all classes and all backgrounds – is into football. It is politically correct now not only for the lads in the pub to discuss 'the back four' but for the Jeremys and Amandas in Fulham, Chelsea and Islington to drink cappuccino and talk about Wenger and

Vieira and Vialli. Football has reformed itself socially upwards; now we have football clubs making spectacular gains on the stock market, investor-owned clubs and cosmopolitan teams. We even have foreign managers speaking better English than the English managers, and in our self-mocking way we rather like that, too. Doesn't that just prove, eh, how educated they are on the continent, and what philistines we are?

True, the working class may have lost out to the television companies; true, season tickets may cost £500 to £800; true, the chants on the terraces may have lost a bit of their bite (well, there aren't any terraces); but it is definitely OK for Articulate Middle England to wear a club scarf, to like football and to talk about the game as if it is a fit topic for intelligent company. Success and winning and spending serious money on it are clearly fine in adult life and on the adult football pitch, but you must not translate that to schools.

Let me get personal on this.

The most competitive person I have ever played swingball against was my daughter. She hit it as if her life depended on it. It was swingball to the death. It was the same hitting a tennis ball. It was the same catching a cricket ball. She had the killer instinct, and she loved it. Sadly, when she went to her state secondary school competitive sport dropped out of her life. By fifteen she played no hockey or tennis. In her case it was not that the school offered no games; she could have played but there was little pressure. To give up sport was too easy: a chat about life and a coffee and a cigarette in a warm café was much more attractive. OK, in her case, then, it was her fault, but I don't think sport should be that easily marginalised. Not only her body, but an important part of her personality was not exercised.

As for myself, some terms I have spent more hours coaching teams and working with actors than I have spent in the classroom — or so it seems. In doing so I have come to know my pupils (and they me) in a way the classroom does not easily allow. I have seen them in situations academic life cannot provide and I have been able to take that knowledge back into the classroom.

For many years I coached and refereed rugby. For a few years I coached hockey (well, sort of). Throughout my teaching time I have coached cricket. What finally finished me off in rugby was the shouting, the sense of impotence, the bulging eyeballs, the incipient heart attack and (worst of all) the constant temptation to harangue. When things went wrong I began to suspect that not only were my players weak (as some of them might well have been) but that the opposition referees were cheats. (Well, let's face it, some of them were.) What finished me off in hockey was the boredom.

With cricket it is different. You can talk quietly, discuss tactics, plot strategies, think long term, point out technical flaws and enjoy the slowly unfolding psychological war each Saturday. Did I say 'enjoy'? Enjoy the feeling of a hot knife slowly turning and twisting in your entrails? No, not enjoy exactly, but feel every kind of emotion, frustration, elation, humiliation, loss, laughter and blank despair. And, standing uncomfortably dressed in my double standards on the higher moral ground, I have tried to teach my teams to eschew triumphalism and to avoid sulking. (Resist quoting Kipling's 'If' here . . . 'If' quote resisted.)

Come the summer term, with exams looming, and pupils can easily and understandably claim academic pressure. Certainly there has never been more pressure on pupils than in this mad module/course work/final examination era. Given this, the temptation to drift away from sport is even stronger, and should be even more strongly resisted. Pupils are every bit as likely to succeed in exams, if not likely to do even better, if they take some exercise and enjoy sport. They may need the change of scene, the change of focus, the fresh air, the physical

exercise, the fun and the farce, and – above all – the chance
to forget themselves in play.

For the teacher, selecting a side and choosing a captain are
essentially no different from sorting through application
forms, coming up with a short list and deciding, after interviews, who'll be the next person to join your department.
You're assessing people. You are trying to decide who you want
on board, what they will be like under pressure, will they rise
to the occasion, prepare properly, encourage others and come
up trumps. Or do you sense their heads will drop, that they're
a piss-weak group who will turn nasty when the wheels come
off? It's a human judgement.

I am a team player. Whenever I fill in one of those management questionnaires to establish the kind of person I am
(Leader, Innovator, Ideas Man, Serial Killer) I always come
out slap in the middle of the team player mark range. So I
have a vested interest in finding and understanding the elusive chemistry which makes a department or a team more
than the sum of its parts. As a sports coach or a head of department, you often wonder if you are asking too much or not
enough. To one person, what you are demanding may seem
out of proportion; to another, it may be a very necessary
stretching.

You should ask a great deal of the team and of the young,
but not too much. Ah, there's the rub, there's the judgement,
that's the tricky bit. You should ask a great deal of yourself, but
not too much. And that is an even more difficult judgement.
Don't behave like a god. Don't expect perfection from them or
from you. You must ensure it does not become too much for
your pupils, and you must resist the temptation to live vicariously through them. You can't and you shouldn't take the
passion and the blood out of sport, but as a teacher you must
maintain self-control and respect for the opposition. It matters
but it mustn't matter too much. Of course on one level it is

only a game, but when you're coaching or playing a game it's only fun if you take it seriously. If it simply doesn't matter, why play at all? Go for a walk instead, as I often do.

Winning is not everything. Sometimes winning is too easy. What gives me the greatest satisfaction is to see the individual and collective effort, the mutual support, the refusal to give in, and a group of players who don't hide. I have sometimes seen that best exemplified in defeat, especially in close games against superior opposition, with everyone fighting in the conviction that it can still be won against all the odds and giving his best until the last moment. After watching that, far from the sick loser feeling in the pit of your stomach, you feel appropriate pride.

Take games and coaching games away from my teaching life and you would take away so much: the conversations, the self-expression and self-discovery, the comedy, the hours of application, the crazy highs, the injustices, the lucky escapes and the insights into human nature. That's why I've done it, and why I believe competitive sport should be a part of every child's school days. As an experience it beats the hell out of much else that's on offer.

And every now and then you have a game so sensational, so exciting in its gut-wrenching involvement, that it makes up for the cold days and the hours of motorway travel and the batting collapses and the dropped catches, and when you come in the front door at 8.30 on a Saturday night and drop your scorebook and punch the air – you're young again, and like all teachers, still something of a child at heart. If there wasn't a bit of that in us it wouldn't be much good.

28
Walking Away

It is eighteen years ago, almost to the day –
A sunny day with the leaves just turning,
The touch-lines new-ruled – since I watched you play
Your first game of football, then, like a satellite
Wrenched from its orbit, go drifting away

Behind a scatter of boys. I can see
You walking away from me towards the school
With the pathos of a half-fledged thing set free
Into a wilderness, the gait of one
Who finds no path where the path should be.

That hesitant figure, eddying away
Like a winged seed loosened from its parent stem,
Has something I never quite grasp to convey
About nature's give-and-take – the small, the scorching
Ordeals which fire one's irresolute clay.

I have had worse partings, but none that so
Gnaws at my mind still. Perhaps it is roughly

Saying what God alone could perfectly show –
How selfhood begins with a walking away,
And love is proved in the letting go.

C DAY LEWIS (1904–72)

29
Father And Son

The Child is father of the Man;
And I could wish my days to be
Bound each to each by natural piety.

WORDSWORTH, 'My heart leaps up'

Some of Wordsworth's best lines, the truth of which grows more each year in my heart and mind: what we are and what we do, our experiences as a child, give birth to the fully grown man. 'And Wordsworth's gift was often granted,' Hugh Sykes Davies wrote. 'What Wordsworth had seen and felt as a child continually entered into what he saw and felt as a man, casting over his later vision a power which is only to be understood in terms of its relation with earlier visions, and with the words which linked it all together.'

So, for a Wordsworthian like me – Wordsworth fan or Wordsworth groupie doesn't quite catch the flavour – it had to happen. My father taught me; the day would come when I taught my son. In 1991, a full forty years after I sat in my father's primary school class, E. T. Smith's name appeared on one of my set lists. I could easily have asked for my class to be changed: some teachers don't like the idea of having their own children sitting in amongst the other pupils. They feel it unhelpfully mixes the professional and the personal, putting an extra strain on already difficult public and private roles. I can understand the force of that argument, and as I had seen so much of my children I wondered if this hands-on move was perhaps one move too many.

Would things at home become claustrophobically over-heated? Was there a danger that we already knew far too much about each other, and that as he watched me perform it would be difficult for me and for him to be normal? Worse, would my double standards be exposed? In fact it's even more complex than that because – perhaps more than all other subjects – teaching English is neither formal nor informal, being at its best a kind of public intimacy, a kind of private formality. Would his presence therefore affect the natural way in which I acted and performed in class? And would the class's responses differ because he was there?

A further anxiety about having him in my class was based on what I had seen happen to sons of other teaching colleagues. Far from currying favour in various ways or taking advantage of their parents' position, some of these children tended to go even further inside themselves. They became too head-down, too low-profile. If anything they made their presence insufficiently felt. 'If I do this or that,' their body-language said, 'I'll be letting Mum or Dad down. So I'll say nothing.' It's a very sweet and touching aim to protect your parents but that is not a natural mind-set for an adolescent in school hours.

Mind you, far from being overawed or too low-profile in his first year at school – the year before I taught him as a fourteen-year-old – Ed's quick mind, quick tongue and assertiveness in debate had been more than sufficiently felt. No one had accused him of lacking confidence. So I asked him if he was at all uneasy about the prospect of my teaching him. He wasn't.

'Fine,' he said, 'if it's OK by you.'

It was OK by me.

In so far as I ever taught my daughter Becky it was, as I have already said, through conversation from day one, from talking to her in her pram, then by leaving books on her bed, through walks and phone calls and letters: this went on throughout her schooldays, through Oxford, and it remains the case now. I haven't done any of this to 'be a good dad'. I've done it because I enjoyed it. Sometimes at school and at university I did talk to her in a serious and extended way about a book or a period of literary history, but it was never formal instruction.

In more recent years it has become a matter of mutual encouragement, of sharing perceptions and of sharpening each other's responses. She has, for example, discussed and criticised the development of this book with me from the first draft to the final copy. As so often happens with parents and teachers, you end up being the one learning.

Teaching Ed did not prove a problem. I would not pretend I ever forgot he was there, that's an unlikely scenario with any son and certainly with Ed, but I just got on with it. I taught in my usual way and played my usual games; I found I enjoyed his presence in class as much as I have always enjoyed it elsewhere. It became, I suppose, a bit easier to teach him each week. Besides, it was a class full of interesting and challenging pupils – one of the best I have taught – and there was always plenty of edge in the air. As well as the smell of food and sweets.

Clever though they were – to digress for just a moment – I have to say they were clueless, quite clueless, about eating. Few things are more mind-bogglingly insulting to a teacher than incompetent eating in class, and Ed's class was no exception. You are, for example, exploring a Shakespearean soliloquy or analysing a difficult poem or defining a subtle distinction between the meaning of two words, yet it is assumed, even by the highly intelligent people involved in this demanding discourse, that they can open a packet of crisps or sweets in their pocket (right in front of you as you stand there stretching your mind as well as stretching theirs), and that they can do all this without you, the teacher, who is now suddenly brain-dead, noticing anything at all. It is assumed, don't ask me why, that while this noisy crackling-opening-unpeeling-chomping action is being performed, the teacher does not see this, and the teacher does not hear this, and that if the teacher *does* catch the eye of the eater mid-chomp all the eater has to do by way of deceiving the brain-dead one is either:

(i) to look choirboy-angelic; or

(ii) to seem lost in eye-rolling master-pleasing concentra-tion, a concentration on the soliloquy which is suddenly so intense that it also requires prolonged philosophical inspec-tion of the ceiling; or

(iii) to smile a cheek-bulging rictus-smile which is guaran-teed to make the teacher think, 'Gosh, what a nice civilised bunch this lot are!'

There is, though, a plus side to all this for the teacher, which I am happy to pass on. Once I smell/hear/see that we are into eating mode (and since I am not stupid it is usually all three of my senses which are at work, especially my sense of smell, for who even at a hundred yards' distance cannot smell prawn-cocktail-flavoured crisps?) I like to pretend that I have not noticed all this going on, to pretend that I am indeed the sad person they are basing their conduct on, and that I did not hear that telltale rattle of the packet or the firing ping of a can opening (the latter usually accompanied by a strangulated cough).

Rattle!

Crunch!

Crackle!

Ping!

Chomp!

And me? Did I hear anything?

No, boys, I didn't hear a thing.

That's how daft I am, boys.

Then, just as the would-be eater is moving the crisp or half-rolling the sweet slowly up his body, and all this time he is of course keeping the crisp or the sweet so close to his body that it requires a creepily contorted horror film hand movement, and just before he has – smiling innocently – popped it into the corner of his mouth behind widely spread fingers, I am faced with two delicious options: either to ask him a direct question the split second before it goes into his mouth (and see how he is going to abort the pre-planned eating, not to mention unravel his weird body position) or to ask him a direct question just after it is in his mouth (and see how his mouth and throat deal with that choking, eye-popping problem).

In the evenings Ed and I used to enjoy reliving all this, and other silly moments, as seen from our different classroom perspectives. He would then move it up a gear, move it away from a laugh and back to academic business, complaining, 'But why did you say that to x? You don't believe that,' or, 'You don't really think much of poet z, do you, be honest, not really?'

At that stage (he was only fourteen) I did not explain to him that in teaching, as in any other business, there has to be a bit of bullshit. Deciding how much, and at what stage, to tell a child something is a tricky one. Some things, however, weren't tricky at all. If he ever, for example, accused me in private of undermarking him and overmarking the others, I would retaliate in public by giving him the part of the second servant or telling him to read out the stage directions; and once or twice I had to ask my wife to go up to his room and tell him his English teacher had all the essays handed in on time except one.

Strangely enough, it was at about this time that my father

began to lose his vitality and sharpness of mind. He was no longer capable of doing The Times crossword. After a small stroke, his handwriting – for so long his pride and joy – went haywire, and he couldn't even write his name on cheques. Though he lived on for a while I was increasingly aware that year, the year when I was teaching Edward, that the Smith father–son teaching relationship had come full circle. I arrived in the world. Dad taught me. Ed arrived. I taught him. Dad was leaving us. We were handing it on.

While worrying about my father, I sometimes looked along the rows of faces in my classroom and caught in Ed some amused gesture, some expressive movement of his hands and eyes which reminded me so strongly of my father. I can still see my father standing at the front of the class in 1951, teaching me; I can still see Ed sitting in my class in 1991. Some things endure. All families and fathers know that feeling. It can take your breath away.

While most parents, naturally enough, are very concerned about their children's development, they only become seriously interested in 'Education with a capital E' when their own children are going through it. Those are the years in which parents fully tune in to the educational debate and look carefully at the current practice in a particular school. They focus intensely on what happens to the child who matters most in the world: their child. Before school age, and once their children have left school, they tend not to engage. There is nothing surprising in such self-interest.

In my more cynical moments, though, I am sometimes amused to spot a particular kind of parental attitude in a particular kind of parent. (You may have encountered this one yourself.) In the years before their children first go to school, I often hear these parents say, 'We're very happy with the local schools. What's good enough for everyone else is good enough for us. We wouldn't be seen dead sending our children anywhere else.' Fine. When the child is about eight or nine, however, the tune changes to 'Although *in principle* we are very against sending our children anywhere other than to the local school, our son/daughter is a very bright and lively little thing and, sadly, he/she is not really being stretched, and we've looked into it, but, sadly, it seems there just aren't the schools around here to bring out the best in him/her. We are absolutely convinced there are loads of good schools available in other parts of the country, but, sadly, not here, so although it's very against our principles we have decided . . .' Ten years or so later, after their children have got their good grades and have gone off to university, the tune reverts to 'Looking back on it, we feel the children would have done just as well if we had saved our money and left them where they were.'

No, mustn't be cynical, but certainly my interest in the education my school was offering its pupils sharpened when my son was going through it. That class I taught, for example, like so many I have taught before and since, contained many clever people, but when Edward was my pupil for a year I thought more than I had ever done about how we catch and hold sharp minds.

At the very same time, as luck would have it, the school itself was also examining this question: six of my colleagues, anxious that we should not bore the brightest, formed together to discuss the issue. (Yes, another committee, but one of the better ones.) The teachers were of all ages in the profession and came from a full range of subject areas. After fourteen meetings they published their conclusions, some of which I have raided in the next few pages. If they complain of plagiarism I will buy them a drink; anyway, I submitted my own ideas to them and I have made what follows far more personal than their report.

*

Without a doubt, one of the maddest and most unchallenged assumptions in education is that clever pupils do not need teaching. 'She's so bright, she doesn't need any help', 'He's so clever all you need to do is step aside and wave him on through', 'Teaching clever kids is so easy, you just go in and throw a few ideas around and they teach themselves', 'If my classes were full of bright children every day would be Christmas', 'They'll just cruise it, leave them alone', 'Anyone can teach clever pupils, it's the not-so-able we should be concentrating on', 'They've got so much going for them, that top set, they've got a head start and a following wind, they don't need any more', 'She'll be all right, she's got so much natural ability, she motivates herself' . . .

Over the years I've heard all these, and more. It wouldn't be so shocking if they were remarks you picked up in the wider world, in the good old anti-intellectual British world, but all the ones I have quoted above are commonly heard in schools, schools of all kinds. You can write off some of them as mistakenly woolly and soft-headed, but there is often a disturbing undercurrent of animus: these clever kids must be punished in some way, held back, pulled back from the front runners, they're arrogant, they must be encouraged to stop showing off and learn to settle contentedly in the big mass of runners we can now see from our helicopter camera, yes, there they are, coming over London Bridge, thousands of them, chatting happily amongst themselves, all settled in nicely behind the breakaway group, they're running along for the fun of it, it doesn't matter what position they come, does it, this is not about times or competition, it's the participation, it's the joining-in that matters.

Rubbish.

If we want to stop our most gifted pupils going off track, as so many do (especially gifted boys), we must address their intellectual development and needs. Top teachers of a certain kind, special teachers, make the difference at a critical time for top and special pupils. Interestingly, the phrase 'special needs' is only used in education for those with learning difficulties. There are, of course, special needs at every level. Different pupils may click with different teachers, but it is extremely unlikely that brilliant pupils will click with a teacher of average intelligence who never touches overdrive, let alone one who is philosophically or politically opposed to that intellectual shift. I find it sobering, if not humbling, to realise how important our lessons are with our most gifted pupils, how significant they might prove, and to wonder how our exchanges with them may guide or inspire them to reach out more confidently for an intellectually exciting future.

Teachers should remember that their classrooms may well contain pupils who have much sharper, quicker and deeper minds. Even within the A-grade band there may well be an individual or a considerable group who are not firing. They may be doing 'very well' without even bothering. It is often the case that schools and examination boards set work and examinations that do not require that firing. The students get top grades without being stretched. And while the published results look fine on paper, the pupils remain unexcited.

Is that an achievement?

So, for those parents and for those teachers who are striving for a better performance from the most able children, I would suggest the following advice. I make no apology that the ten points sound so simple, nor that I have made some of them earlier in this book. A teacher has to repeat some simple statements.

1. Numero uno (ironically) is . . . do not labour a point. If an idea is relatively easy and established do not spell it out. They've already got it. The most able can fill in the gaps. Watch out for yawns. If they yawn and look out of the

window your intellectual bad manners – painting by numbers and joining up the dots – are being punished by their
social bad manners.

2. Refuse to be dominated by the syllabus. Much of our teaching must go wider and deeper than that. With the tendency
for examination boards to become ever more prescriptive
and wordy it is only too easy to spend the whole year in
that mode, ensuring solemn and lengthy attention is paid
to the obvious. Do not tolerate tedium. When a question is
trivial, recognise it as such. Syllabuses are set with the average in mind. While much of the educational establishment
used to be tuned to the standard of the able, the opposite is
now more likely. Do not be trammelled by the inappropriate nature of the demands. Stretch the brightest minds.
Do not dumb down.

3. Expectation is the key. Try to expect and demand excel-
lence. Many pupils will then go the extra mile. There is an
element of flattery in all this.

4. Demand oral work of the highest standard. It is all too
tempting to settle for a notion of accessibility, a radio-
phone-in-speak, sort-of kind-of stuff, where it's sort of in to
kind of take a long time to, you know, say something, I
mean you are articulate deep down, but the thing is, I don't
like to kind of use the full range, you know, when I talk in
class because it's kind of off-putting and up myself if I sort
of sound like I'm showing off. Know what I mean? Well,
don't do it. OK?

Articulation, thinking and speaking well under pressure,
is so important. Pupils should be encouraged and prompted
to think quickly on their feet. This will not only make the
lessons more lively, but also more exciting for the teacher

and the class. The discussion, the dialectic method, the Socratic journey may well go down paths into areas not envisaged or planned. If so, that's wonderful. A good pupil is often able to solve problems orally, especially when confronted with unfamiliar questions. And answers, of course, are themselves open to further question.

5. Draw ideas out of pupils as much as possible. Don't hand them the answers. Let them find interesting twists and ragged edges. Let them feel their own ideas flowing. This helps to build up what I like to call 'intellectual muscle', which might be seen as another way of describing independence of mind.

6. All pupils at all levels need sensitive support and encouragement. This is just as true of the very clever, yet this support is often (and to my mind curiously) denied them. Encourage them to hold on to each other in an argument. Don't discourage or ever be tempted to mock those able students who are just a little slower than the best.

7. When pupils see through a somewhat simplistic argument we should be willing to respond to it with the truth, however hard that may be. Don't fudge it. Don't pretend you have already explained it if you haven't. Discovery, a science colleague told me, consists of seeing what everyone has seen and thinking what no one has thought. So, rethink, abandon, change track, set off again. Often, I have to admit, I am not too sure where we are going, but I am backing us to get somewhere. I am a great believer in the long-term game. I see myself as on a journey with them.

This is all very demanding (especially if you have allowed yourself to become too exhausted to think), very demanding but very rewarding, and the reward is the thrill of engaging with gifted young minds.

From their own days as pupils many teachers may recall that they often did not feel the ideas being put to them stood up. It may then have been considered rude to point this out. No teacher today should relish that deferential attitude. It is possible to be irreverent of easy views and still disagree in a civilised way. A high boredom threshold does not go hand in hand with good education. Do not put up with mediocrity for the sake of a negotiated peace. Run the risk of an arrogant response. It is surely better than a dishonest discussion conducted in an atmosphere of indifference.

If a pupil continues to go on at length, to hold the floor in a wrong-headed way, I recommend a line used by one of my most courteous but tough-minded colleagues, 'Yes, very interesting, and thank you for that. One to pursue elsewhere, I think, and in your own time.'

8. Just as important as a lively, peppery feel is its counterpoint, a spirit of quiet attentiveness. Try to develop an atmosphere in which pupils can enjoy reflection, recollection and the company of their own considered thoughts. You often see more from a slow-moving boat. So much of our educational practice is based on buttons and impact, on quick hits and fast responses, on zapping in and zapping out. Much of this masquerades as thought. Look closer; think more.

9. Fight against the tyranny of fashion and relevance. The study of literature, to take my own subject, is not mainly to be promoted or developed or even introduced on the grounds that it is all about us. Often it is to be encouraged precisely because it is not about us but about other peoples,

other worlds, old and new, other beliefs, other ages which may be as remote from us in some respects as they are similar to us in others.

10. And for number ten we must return to Wordsworth. Encourage even your best pupils to understand that however hard and deep you look beneath the surface of the water, what you see is always partly blurred by the reflection of yourself, by the surface image of your own face as you hang out of the boat. It is the same when we, as parents or teachers, examine our pasts. You can, so easily, see things in the water that are not really there. This recognition – I am speaking here mostly of enquiry in the arts – moves us towards intellectual humility of the highest and most appropriate kind. No one has ever expressed this profoundly simple truth better than Wordsworth in these lines from Book Four of *The Prelude*:

> *As one who hangs down-bending from the side*
> *Of a slow-moving boat, upon the breast*
> *Of a still water, solacing himself*
> *With such discoveries as his eye can make*
> *Beneath him in the bottom of the deeps,*
> *Sees many beauteous sights – weeds, fishes, flowers,*
> *Grots, pebbles, roots of trees, and fancies more,*
> *Yet often is perplexed and cannot part*
> *The shadow from the substance, rocks and sky,*
> *Mountains and clouds, from that which is indeed*
> *The region, and the things which there abide*
> *In their true dwelling, now is crossed by gleams*
> *Of his own image, by a sunbeam now,*
> *And motions that are sent he knows not whence*
> *Impediments that make his task more sweet.*
>
> *The Prelude*, IV, 247–261

This is where objectivity and subjectivity meet, the world and you, the substance and the shadow. If you forget or reject everything else that I have written about teaching able pupils, please reread the Wordsworth. Even better, learn it. I'll test you on it the next time we meet.

30
Examinations (And The Course-Work Conspiracy)

Every teacher, especially a teacher who writes a book, surely has to say something about examinations?

Does he? Do they?

Well, they go hand in hand, don't they, teachers and examinations, that's what it's all about, tests and teachers, results and re-sits, re-marks and appeals, soft options and sensible decisions, marks and masters, numbers up in computing and general studies while chemistry falls, schools accuse the boards, schools are accused by the boards, state schools attack the independents, independents say traditional methods pay dividends, commentators attack lenient marking and the manipulation of entries, are standards lowering or improving, should our praise for those who do well be more restrained or more celebratory, are results used as marketing tools, schools in league tables fight each other tooth and claw, how do we view the successses and how do we come to terms with the suicides?

Meanwhile, faced with the continuing fall in graduate science teachers, the government offers the recruiting temptation of £5,000 'golden hullos'. Not exactly a firm City golden handshake, more a sweaty, limp touch, but who can afford to be superior?

When I was a boy it was the 11-plus and the School Certificate, then it was O levels and CSEs and A levels, and then it was GCSEs and A levels, and now it's five of these in the Lower Sixth and four of those in the last year at school, or is it As or A2s or AS . . . But, look, if I go on it will be out of date before this book is published. Put it this way, you can be sure they're working on it right now, the men in suits, and you can be sure it's going to be different next year: it has been, in one way or another, every year for the last fifteen.

When I was young, assuming you (to use a sexy terrn) 'went all the way' in education – and money and education (we are told) are now very sexy topics – there were only three hurdles, three big exam years: at eleven, at sixteen and at eighteen. Putting on one side all the primary school testing, there is now a serious examining element in most of the secondary years. For those pupils between fifteen and eighteen there are exams or examination equivalents, i.e. modules or course-work components, every year.

Thank God it's not me taking all these exams, I can hear you say; thank God it's not me teaching all these, you can hear most teachers say before they leave. Not only the pupils but the teachers live in fear of the results. Thank God I'm getting out, teachers confide to you with a desperate smile, before I have to get used to the latest round of changes, I really can't face it any more . . .

This is a personal book, a sort-of autobiography, with no pretensions to be a State-Of-The-Art-State-Of-The-Education-We're-In (kind of) book, so I don't intend writing about the curriculum or giving an overview of the national examination picture, but I do want to say something about a development within examinations which worries me – and worries all the teachers I have ever spoken to on this issue.

Once again, as in so many areas of education, it is not easy to talk honestly about this in print without the feeling that one is fouling one's own nest, that one is letting down one's profession or upsetting one's pupils or colleagues. In terms of a quiet life, it would be easier for me if I did not say this.

But here we go.

What is the thing most on the mind of sixteen-year-olds? According to the magazine I was reading in my hairdresser's the other day, it is sex – to which their minds and instincts return on average every thirty-seven seconds. A specially selected team has researched this in depth. They are wrong. It is not sex that obsesses many middle teenagers, though that flits in and out of focus. What obsesses them is another dreaded c word: course-work.

For four years running, from fifteen to eighteen, just when their emotional life is exploding, just when they are widely supposed and widely suspected to be experiencing for the first time the forbidden fruit, they are thinking about demands and pressures of an entirely different kind. In every classroom and on every corridor they are being told, 'Your English course-work is due in on Monday', 'The deadline for your geography project is Tuesday, and any work handed in after that day WILL NOT COUNT', 'You are reminded that your drama course-work must be in by Wednesday at the latest (NO EXTENSIONS)', 'Your biology assessment . . .'

– Does it *have* to be in on Monday, sir?
– Yes.
– Sir!
– Monday I said, and Monday it is. I've said Monday a thousand times.
– I put mine under your door last Thursday.
– No, you didn't.
– I left it on your desk on Friday.
– No, you didn't.
– Can I hand it in tomorrow then?

– No, we all agreed Monday. We've been through all this!

– But my geography project is due in tomorrow.

– Tough.

– Yeah, but he goes ape if it's late, he really does.

– So do I.

– No, you don't, sir. He's scary, he won't budge, he never does . . . but you know what we're going through, you do, sir, you know how much we have to hand in. You're reasonable, sir. You don't think your subject is the only subject.

– Yes, I do.

– Not in the same way, sir.

– It won't work, sorry.

– Is it a real deadline then, sir?

– What do you mean, 'a real deadline'?

– Matt Davies rang up the board, and they're not due in, the marks and folders, for another six weeks.

– The cheeky sod.

– So, what's all the rush?

– Well, that's the board's deadline, but we have an earlier deadline, all schools do, it's an internal matter. A departmental matter.

– Why?

– To do some moderation. We all have our own deadlines. For internal moderation. We all sit down together, it takes hours, you've no idea. Comparing one class against another. Taking scripts from the top, middle and lower grades. Making sure we've got it right. Making sure you're all being treated absolutely fairly. Applying the criteria. Believe it or not, we're professionals, and all this takes time.

– But you sit on our work for six weeks?

– Look, I'm not the head of department, get it in on Monday or else! Is that clear enough? Monday!

– There's another thing. I didn't want to tell you, sir, but I feel I should.

– Yes?

– Things aren't too good at home, sir.

– At home?

– They really aren't. I don't know how to tell you.

– Oh, I'm sorry to hear that . . . In what way?

– It's been getting to me. Everything. That's what's made me get behind.

– Look, I really am sorry, but I can't make exceptions.

– The thing is, my father's gone off with someone else, a month ago, it's shattered my mum, I've never seen her like it, she doesn't know what's going on. And my sister's got anorexia.

– Gosh, that's . . . that's tough, that's difficult for you, I can see that . . . Even so, a deadline's a deadline. Your sister, too . . . I'll have a word. I'll . . . see what I can do.

– Would you? Just till Friday, it'll be on your desk on Friday.

– I'll see what my colleagues say. I'll have to clear it with them. But no promises. OK?

– Thanks, sir, thanks a lot.

At some stage in the last thirty years – historians are unclear over the exact date – it was decided that it was unfair to assess a pupil purely on work done under timed examination conditions, i.e. in an examination hall without books. The argument went something like this. An end-of-year examination or an end-of-course examination is unfair because some pupils aren't very good at sitting such an examination. It works against them. Their marks are poor. The examination is inappropriate. It ensures most people feel failures. It doesn't play to everyone's strengths. What happens if they have an off day? What happens if someone has a migraine or is having a period or, as sometimes happens, performs uncharacteristically badly? Far too many candidates (who either freeze on the day or become hot and sweaty and stressed) are doing themselves less than justice. What kind of an educational system is that?

Final, timed, written examinations (the argument ran on) reinforce rote learning and reward those with a good memory for facts. Facts are not the most important thing. (Indeed 'facts' became something of a dirty word. To mock the memory and fact element in education all you had to do was to quote Mr Gradgrind from Dickens's *Hard Times*.) Working on your own is what matters, interpretation is what matters, and interpretation is best delivered at the student's own pace. Would it not be more sensible, more balanced and more fair, to give longer stretches of time to the student, and to allow him to do a significant amount of the course – anything from 10 per cent to 100 per cent – on his own?

Then individual effort would be rewarded. Everyone would have a better, more flexible, more humane opportunity to fulfil his potential. Let's see what the pupil can find in the library, on the internet and in the resource centre, let's see what he can do when he runs the extra mile but does not feel that unnecessary stress, the stress that comes from feeling it is a do-or-die examination day. On hand in the background will be the teacher, sensitive to individual needs, the teacher who knows his pupils so much better than any examination board ever could, there to help with drafts and to encourage and monitor the pupil's progress.

And, of course, some very good course-work has been done. It would be absurd to argue otherwise. Each year I read a number of astonishingly interesting, well-researched and worthwhile pieces and hear my colleagues say the same, though I would have to add that they are usually handed in by those pupils who will also prove to be successful under timed conditions in the examination hall. Nevertheless, some English teachers look back with nostalgia to those few years in the early 1990s when there was 100 per cent course-work – and I can see why. For in those years they themselves were totally in charge of their pupils and could stretch them with courses of their own devising, rather than merely follow the syllabus or fulfil the present GCSE approach of running or dribbling round and round the foothills ticking boxes and passing checkpoints until you are clapped out with boredom. (What about climbing a hill instead, or a mountain, which would mean seeing something worth seeing?) Even though 100 per cent course-work made teachers 100 per cent unpaid examiners, it had some clear advantages for both the teacher and the pupil.

The arguments against course-work can be briefly stated. One point is essentially minor but worth making. Three points strike me as major issues.

The minor point: course-work, in many of its forms, encourages pupils to concentrate on presentation before content. With the ever-growing quality of computers and word-processing there lands on the teacher's desk an ever-growing mound of beautifully bound course-work, with the most stunning title pages, all letters printed in any number of fonts (Times New Roman or Palatino or Impact or Double Bold), all the words spell-checked and formatted, all the pages laminated, all indexed and footnoted, all adding up to under-lined multicoloured mush, much of it bollocks with bullet points, and all worthy of a clear A* for pretty presentation and a clear fail for an absence of presence.

Secondly, the move towards course-work in schools, and towards project-teaching and long essays at university level, means the pupil is told less. The best teachers, in my experi-ence, tell you things. Now the pupil is told less, and yet, paradoxically, the less he is told the more he is being told to think for himself. As he almost certainly does not think anything much, he is forced to reach for the nearest intellectual fashion or to press the nearest button. Which is it to be: what everyone else thinks or writing block or plagiarism? As C. S. Lewis put it, 'We castrate, and then bid the geldings be fruitful.'

Thirdly, far from ensuring a soft landing for the candidates, far from reducing the stress levels on pupils, course-work has increased them. (It surely goes without saying that course-work, with its keep-on-measuring fetish, increases stress on teachers.) My concern here, however, is that too many pupils are stressed for long periods, the stress often building up in waves until they find the demands on them severe. It is not so much the quality of the work expected as the sheer weight, and some of the main weight being carried is made even less bearable because it is so brainless. Faced with teachers all telling them that this piece of work is the equivalent of x per cent of the total examination mark, and all stating or implying that the course-work in their subject is the most urgent, many young people (especially those who are not too well organised) find they cannot cope or – which leads me to my most substantial point – look for other ways to dig themselves out of a hole. If you put unrelenting pressure and a series of deadlines on pupils, that is only to be expected.

Finally, I come to the conspiracy. It is a strange conspiracy and a strange collusion because the parties did not and do not get together in secret and agree on a course of action. But it is understood and it is none the less reprehensible. What I am about to describe is common knowledge and common practice, though teachers would prefer to discuss it only in private. My explanation is based on fifteen years of talking to teachers in all kinds of schools, and to listening to the dedicated teachers who collect and assess course-work at all levels.

Pupils, in the time-honoured way, will get help from any and every source: from their teachers, from other pupils, from their older brothers and sisters, from earlier pupils, from the grapevine, from their parents, and from the internet. Everyone, after all, has a vested interest in the pupil doing good course-work, because it is a significant part of the over-all examination mark. Course-work is an examination, albeit one not taken in the examination hall. However you describe it, it is marks in the bank, it is goodies under the belt.

The pupil wants a high mark, then, and will do anything to get this mark. After all, if it is at GCSE level, these results will be the only ones on his UCAS form and may well decide the offers he is made by universities. He would be foolish not to work at it.

The caring parent wants his child to get a high mark and will help his child in any way possible, fair means or foul. Every parent wants the best for his child, never more so than in today's world. Here is a chance to influence that future by influencing the course-work result.

The caring teacher, aware that his annual results are being scrutinised and that these results may well affect his salary and/or promotion prospects, wants his pupil to get a high mark and will, if need be, rewrite or reshape or help in any way possible. Teachers rewriting course-work is on the increase. It might even already be a national scandal.

The caring head of department, aware that his annual results are being scrutinised and compared with other depart-ments both inside and outside the school, wants all the pupils in his department to do well. These results may well affect his salary and/or promotion prospects.

The caring head of the school, either aware or unaware of these practices, but in any event too busy or too shrewd to be likely to peer too closely, is only too pleased if his school does a little better than last year in all subjects. After all, he has to speak about results to the school, and to the parents, and to the governors and, maybe, even to the press.

It is also, of course, in the interests of the examination boards for everyone to do a little better because examination boards are touting for custom, competing with other boards for schools to join them, and schools shop around to look for the easier boards. That's only common sense. In making their offers to pupils, universities do not distinguish between one board and another.

All of this is unsaid but all of this leads to a significant number of marks being massaged or nudged very gently upwards. Not too many marks and not too much upwards, of course, because that would be too obvious and would arouse suspicion, but just enough to make the significant difference, and in these days when tiny decimal points make all the difference over where your school comes in league tables just enough is enough. If a B grade boundary is, say, 71–80, and you are not sure if a pupil is quite a B grade you don't give a mark just on the borderline, you give a mark three or four up. Then, even if the marks are moderated down by the board, they are unlikely to fall below the grade boundary. Not very difficult, is it?

Ah, but what about moderation? That is where the conspiracy will be exposed. What about the internal and external moderation which will ensure that standards are maintained and that none of this jiggery-pokery can happen? Well, much of the internal moderation is either non-existent or muddled or self-interested or a simple mess, because this internal moderation, as is obvious from the above, tends to be part of the conspiracy.

Most teachers only want the best for their pupils (and for themselves) and will, as it were, beg, steal or borrow for them. It's not so much, then, the authenticity of the pupils' work we should be worried about as the authenticity of the task set and of its marking. Given half a chance, even in any old unimportant internal end-of-term test, teachers will look to mark their own pupils above other classes in the same year group. Who wants to be shown up in front of his colleagues? I don't. Who wants to be exposed as a less good teacher? I don't. And why should it be any different with course-work moderation? As for the external moderation, most experienced teachers have lost all confidence in the process and want no part of it. It is deeply boring and poorly paid and most would rather do without the pittance and enjoy their holidays.

So results go on going up and will go on going up. Not too much, but just enough. This year's GCSE results are the best ever. And the results prove that standards are going up. This year's A-level results are the best ever. This is gratifying. And this good news is a cause for general satisfaction. Well done, boys, and increasingly and in particular, well done, girls.

Each year, every August, I listen to all this on the news and I read it in the papers. I look at the statistics and at the photographs of the happy pupils, usually girls, and I feel happy for them. It is much easier to nod, 'May it happen to you!' When there is so little good news for teachers, who wants to spoil the party? Better results redound to the credit of all pupils, and to the credit of my profession, the profession for which I care above all others. Every year things are 'getting better', and I should be glad, and to question any of it is 'to criticise the teaching profession who are working harder than ever before and to do down the very hard-working youngsters you should be pleased for'.

Every year a decent head will write that to the papers in response to a grumpy traditionalist who dares to doubt the forward march. Listening to this, I always feel very uncomfortable, torn between blowing the whistle and hearing my trumpet blown.

31
Sometimes

Sometimes things don't go, after all,
from bad to worse. Some years, muscadel
faces down frost; green thrives; the crops don't fail,
sometimes a man aims high, and all goes well.

A people sometimes will step back from war;
elect an honest man; decide they care
enough, that they can't leave some stranger poor.
Some men become what they were born for.

Sometimes our best efforts do not go
amiss; sometimes we do as we meant to.
The sun will sometimes melt a field of sorrow
that seemed hard frozen: may it happen for you.

SHEENAGH PUGH

32
Finding The Right Role

And sometimes, indeed increasingly often, I ask myself not only what have I achieved but 'What has it all been about?' Have I done the right thing with my life? Have I played the right role, the right role *for me*? As a casting director of myself did I make the best judgement of my abilities? Did I over- or underplay, did I understretch myself or did I face it? Should I have taken a more centre-stage position or did I come on in the right place at the right time and speak lines with which I felt comfortable?

It is not a truism to say that every aspect of teaching is important and every teacher is important; it is simply true. But in my world – the world of independent schools – there are three key jobs: housemastering, running a department and being a head. Every teacher with whom I have worked would, I imagine, ask himself which of these he wants or intends to be, which he feels cut out for. Sometimes you can tell at a glance which way someone should go or is going. On other occasions the choice is more difficult, the way ahead is misty or the paths in the wood look equally attractive.

In my case, I have faced two big decisions. I was, more than once, offered a housemastership but, even though it would

have helped my family financially, I turned it down. Vital and
central job though it is, indeed the pastoral core, I did not feel
cut out for it. It did not feel me. What is more, any temptation
for me to take the job was based on exactly the wrong motives.
So, even though close friends put pressure on me, saying no
wasn't too difficult. The other two jobs – running a department
and being a head – did interest me. In my mind's eye I have
enjoyed analysing and seeing myself in both those roles, and it
is now time to say what I see as important in the first and, in
the next chapter, to say why I kept away from the second.

All this came to a head on a recent six-week visit to schools in
Western Australia and Victoria: I was talking to classes about
creative writing and I was talking to teachers about the value
of staff development and appraisal, yet in public and private I
was most often pressed about the problems of running a
department. What did I see as the key areas? Could I put my
finger on the man-management issues which I would see as
the most central?

   With a shock I realised that although I had done a key job
for seventeen years of my life, from thirty-three to fifty, and
although I was being asked to describe and analyse what (after
all) I had long felt was the right role for me, I had never
thought about it at all clearly. I have since done so, and have
also taken the opportunity to talk to people in other professions to see how things compare in different walks of life; my
friends tell me these applications are almost universal, so I will
try to answer the question properly now. To give it a neat
look, can I make it ten points?

Running a department

1. *Appointing staff.* A department, in this respect, may be seen
   as a school in miniature. Get the appointments right and it

goes from strength to strength. Appoint the right team and it works in a creative, lively spirit. Such a department, with the saving graces of fun and tolerance, can take any setbacks in its stride. Get the appointments wrong and you live with the problem, a murky problem which causes daily irritation, regular complaints from pupils and parents, delusional and exculpatory justifications, increasing blood pressure and you end up gnashing your teeth and practising the Primal Scream. But it's not, sadly, a Primal Scream that works because a bad appointment often proves beyond cure or therapy or even legal moves. You start to imagine you have discovered a new psychiatric category. Basically you're stuck.

People matter more than resources, more than facilities, more than the size of the classroom or the numbers in the set. Much more. Good colleagues inspire and encourage each other. They pass on what is 'working' for them; bad colleagues keep it to themselves and hope to show up the others. Good colleagues compliment and complement each other, suggest books, articles, radio and TV programmes, films, plays, approaches, strategies and hunches. They swap perceptions of pupils. They keep themselves and they keep each other alive. Such a department is as fulfilled and happy as a hard-pressed group of professionals can ever expect to be. On special days it hums, you feel moments of perfect harmony between your self and your world, and you walk tall.

While the head takes the final decision on an appointment, the view of the head of department is critical. So it should be. It is a joint decision. Heads sometimes do overrule the head of department and go for someone else, possibly even against the whole department's wishes. This is risky, but it does happen. Some heads do not like to be told or crossed. Some heads, isolated and dependent on their purple circle of disciples, do not listen. Or they do listen and they explain, quite fairly, that they have other factors to bear in mind, other aspects to consider; they have a better overall view of the school's professional needs.

Often, though, the head and the head of department do agree on the best candidate, or at least have the difficult but not too painful task of choosing between two or more excellent people. Once, after a disagreement, I did win an argument with the head and persuaded him to appoint someone he thought likely to be a problem. 'You'll regret it,' he said. (He was proved right.) Once the head went against my view and appointed someone I thought would be a disaster. (I was proved right.) Apart from those errors of judgement we did reasonably well.

When interviewing it is essential to take as long as it takes. Don't rush it. A common mistake is to cram the interviews into a busy day, dashing in and out of meetings or classes or games, never allowing yourself the time to focus properly. You must be free to walk and talk, to let the candidate see the department and to take in what's on the walls; you need time to follow up angles and hunches, e.g. to probe whether the candidate is still 'alive in the subject', to find out if there is a sense of humour lurking in there somewhere, or to decide if the applicant is pleasantly self-assured or shading towards being a patronising prat.

For a second opinion, introduce a likely runner to shrewd and helpful colleagues outside the department, while steering such a runner well away from those in the community who would put anyone off joining any school: not always easy as some of the biggest Common Room bores seem socially ever-present. They probably haven't anywhere else to go.

While you don't want to trust too much in first impressions you should never appoint anyone if your gut instinct tells you no. Play an open-minded game. If in doubt, sleep on it. With some candidates, however, you don't have to sleep on it; despite their immaculate CVs they are a very serious disappointment at first sight. 'Oh God, no,' you think as they walk towards you, 'this could be a long half-hour,' and it usually is. You can get your sleep in then.

When writing references most heads, sooner or later, will fail the hypocrisy test. We all have a dark shadow. How much does a head want to keep or want to get rid of a teacher? Will that head tell the truth? The school receiving the reference should remember that these references are sometimes as difficult to crack as the Enigma Code. Many and varied are the underwater games, and the English language is a wonderful thing. Is the other head handsomely writing up the applicant in the hope that he can at long, long last be rid of this thorn in his flesh and so sell on a pup? (No more Primal Screams! In such a case the temptation to bring out the big adjectives must prove almost irresistible.)

Or is the other head putting into his reference little qualifying clauses, inviting the reader to think that these are between-the-lines warning-off noises, when in truth and not very deep down he wants to keep that applicant on his staff? A head knows that if he makes an openly critical observation or strikes a subtly cautionary note, that in itself is usually enough to bury anyone's chances. (A good, if not so subtle, recent example: 'He has that combination of haughtiness and pedantry which gives classics such a bad name.')

It's difficult, reading and decoding references. Phone calls are often helpful to flesh things out or to get closer to the truth; but even then, when you can't look into the other person's eyes, deceptions are practised. On the phone it is quite easy to put on a breezy, straight-talking, straight-up-he's-terrific tone. In such a manner some appalling buffoons are moved onwards and upwards. But what does the selling school care, as long as it is a career conducted elsewhere?

Before leaving the matter of applications, it is always worth taking a final trawl through the whole pile that arrived in the head's office. Have you missed someone? Intellectual snobbery can sometimes lead to the CV of a good candidate being side-lined or binned. Some of the finest teachers on any staff – a point already made – had modest school and university records. They were late developers and natural teachers. Some of the least effective classroom performers, on the other hand, have won every academic prize. At least bear that in mind. Look round your own staff and ask whether some of the outstanding colleagues you have would, given some of the current criteria, even make it on to the short list.

It is easy, but potentially dangerous, to fall into the trap of appointing only people you like or only appointing people like you. It's natural to want people on board with whom you feel comfortable, people who will fit in. They'll drink with you, make you laugh and talk the same language. Who can resist it?

Put it this way, though: team-work is one thing, but cosiness can be bought at a price. Some heads of department like to appoint those who would never challenge or threaten them. It's nice if everyone is nodding, even if you are talking crap. The result, though, is likely to be a second-division department, an underpowered team. While you certainly don't want endless open conflict (it's not a pretty sight watching a head of department and a Young Testosterone Turk locking horns) you equally should be aware of the dangers in too many colleagues all coming from the same mould.

As a head of department you should keep in mind the

needs of all your pupils, just as you acknowledge there are many different ways of teaching your subject. The majority of school pupils, after all, are themselves far from intellectual high-fliers and potential firsts. Who is likely to tune in best with them?

Aim to have colleagues from a variety of backgrounds, with different styles and tastes, and with different political and social perspectives. You don't want everyone banging on about Bartok or Blackburn Rovers. On Election Night you don't want everyone cheering the same party. But, over and above all this, ask yourself the final question, 'If I were a pupil would I want this person teaching me?' . . . Then, if you feel the chemistry will work, back your intuition, back your hunch.

2. *Deciding the departmental timetable.* After appointing staff this is the biggest decision. Here you most openly reveal your hand as a head of department. You are deciding not only the overall picture but the precise daily nature of the job that all your colleagues will be doing: who teaches whom, each workload, who takes on the problem areas, how many lessons, how big the sets, who shares with whom, etc. The head of department cuts the cake and there is a clear judgement being made in the cutting and to whom he hands out the pieces.

No head of department should take all the icing himself. Teachers are quick to compare workloads, to assess the nature of each class and to spot the strategems. You are not running a ship of fools. Some heads of department, for fear of offending, give out an equal share to each, each teacher taking a top set, a middle set and – we can't say 'low' – a less able set. Though a clear winner in the decency stakes and rooted in an honourable tradition, don't do that either. It presupposes all members of your department are the same. All hair shirt, a few HoDs (I'm getting fed up with typing the whole phrase) take on all the least attractive bits. 'More weight,' they cry, lying under a pile of stones, 'put another pile on me.' This martyr-doormat mentality may lead them to heaven but it is a shambles here on earth.

The right and only approach is to give each teacher the right timetable for him or her, or as close as you can get to that within the timetable's constraints. You may be lucky enough to have all your teachers capable of teaching well at all levels, but I doubt it.

If you want teachers sharing sets (usually in the A-level years) try to pick complementary pairs, e.g. a young, inexperienced teacher with a seasoned professional, or someone strong in one specialist area with someone strong elsewhere, or avoid putting two drama specialists together. Ironically and unjustly you sometimes are forced, as a HoD, into giving your least effective teacher the 'easiest' timetable, or at least the timetable with the least potential for damage, while you lean yet again on your strong all-rounders to carry more than their fair share. I never found a way round that. Dull teachers tend not to be sacked.

As with interviewing, all this planning and thinking takes hours; but, as with interviewing, get it wrong and you're stuffed. Being stuffed every day for a year is painful. As a matter of courtesy and as a test of character, the HoD should discuss with each colleague next year's proposed timetable. He should not drop them into pigeonholes on the first day of the summer holidays and run away. (Mind you, I've done that.)

3. *Give a lead yourself.* You may not be the cleverest in your department, but you must live your subject by reading,

doing research, going to conferences, and developing your creative and critical mind. For your pupils and for your colleagues you *are*, in a sense, your subject.

4. *The everyday level*. This starts with being first in to the department each morning (unless you've got a nutter who likes to be in at six); be there to open up, to check it is tidy, occasionally perhaps to ask the cleaners about the general state in which the rooms are left, and to be a welcoming presence for other teachers and for early pupils. Everyone notices and appreciates this. (Well, to be honest, they don't, but do it anyway.) In a non-proprietorial sense it then becomes your place and your ground. It may also prove the right moment to thank or praise, or the best opportunity to speak to a worried or overstretched colleague. Our profession has more than its fair share of these.

On an even gentler scale, putting your head round a door or giving a little wave can lift a teacher's mood and bring a smile. Sometimes I left a colleague a scurrilous or silly note, a private line if you like, and I enjoyed the thought of the teacher's face as the note was opened with the class all sitting there. In this most human of jobs, the human touch is part of your leadership, and the human touch may also help you to win much bigger battles that may lie ahead. In a world dominated by market-led-assessment-target-speak, human touch remains a vital dimension.

5. *Delegation*. Delegation is a fine thing. The HoD cannot do everything and should not do everything. Colleagues like to be trusted, and like to be entrusted with the opportunity to prove themselves. They like to feel – and sometimes should be given – an area for which they are solely responsible. An appropriately delegated department will have more energy.

Some HoDs, understandably, find it almost impossible to let go, believing they can do it all so much better than anyone else. 'Oh, leave it to me. I'll do it. I don't mind.' (At least it will then be properly done.) We've all said or thought that. It's silly.

Equally, HoDs should not delegate so much that it looks less like empowering others and more like off-loading the nasty bits. Colleagues then start asking themselves – and that is only one short step from asking each other – 'Um, er, excuse me, forgive me, I know this may sound disloyal . . . but what exactly is the HoD doing for his money?'

We're back to that big, boring word: balance.

6. *In-service training and staff development.* For many years I did none of the first, and for even more years I was never reviewed. I received no professional guidance at all beyond an informal chat. This was not, I hope, a result of institutionalised complacency but it was parochial. True, I was lucky with my heads and deputy heads, but I strongly support the formal insistence on appraisal now operating in most schools. I also take it as obvious that all members of the department should, at some stage, go on courses and attend conferences.

In my late fifties I have learnt new things about myself and about how to do my job. It has made me want to improve and to listen more. Know-alls are bores. Even though I have been giving a lot of advice in this book, it is my seven years of co-ordinating staff review and appraisal that have led me to writing these pages. While no system of development is perfect, and all schemes have their critics, professionally organised review brings colleagues together, face to face, in a formal setting, with the HoD and the headmaster centrally involved. Private dinner parties, pub chats, huddles in the corner of the staff room, walks around the grounds and late-night telephone calls cannot do this.

7. *Visit other schools.* Give talks in other schools. Attend meetings in other schools. Whatever the travelling involved, and however tiring the day seems in prospect, it is invariably invigorating. Nick all the best ideas on offer. What are they doing which is more interesting than your practices? Too many teachers are defensive and fearful of change. Discuss your problems and anxieties with other HoDs. This can save you from feeling embattled.

Arrange for others to visit you: writers, academics, actors, travelling companies, whatever. These will lift and enliven your pupils and your department. However little you pay, pay you must. Not to do so is insulting. When I visit another school to talk about my writing I expect to be paid. Do not trade on good will or try to get away with it. It is not a privilege for them to visit your school, though some schools seem to proceed on that pompous basis. It is a professional matter. Unless they specifically say they do not want to be, outside speakers must be paid.

8. *Watch other teachers teach:* sometimes for interest, sometimes to be inspired, sometimes to remind yourself of the quality of those you work with, sometimes just for the fun of it. I am not talking here about team teaching, though I always enjoy that, but about watching e.g. scientists and sports teachers at work. Chris Stone, the cricket professional at Tonbridge for eight years, effectively ran a master class for any young teacher: his punctuality, his turn-out, his attention to detail, his insights, his strategies for individual and group improvement, and the sense he sometimes gave of not having inexhaustible patience with those who would not listen.

As a young teacher in 1972 I was asked by the head-master to write the school prospectus. This required finding out everything I could about how the school worked and, where possible, photographing it. In doing all this my respect for my colleagues in all departments shot up. It was amazing what was going on: up until that point I had lived in the sure knowledge that the English Department was the centre of the school.

The prospectus went well and I only got into trouble once. That was for suggesting the caption to go under a wonderful wide-angled photo of the inside of the school chapel. For various technical reasons we had to photograph it on a slow exposure when the building was empty. The head rejected my suggested caption, 'Voluntary Chapel'.

9. *Departmental meetings*. Frustrating though they can be, you do need regular meetings, preferably timetabled. There needs to be a clear agenda and a crisp atmosphere. A good meeting enlivens and strengthens morale. The HoD should at all costs, however, avoid the resentment that can build up when the truth is scrupulously avoided or predictably blurred. Even so, the value of such gatherings outweighs the sense of frustration that all colleagues feel when so little has been settled.

Some teachers make it all the more difficult for the HoD by bad body language or by contributing next to nothing, preferring to talk tough before and after rather than during the event. Sitting like statues, they remind me of the lines in *The Merchant of Venice*:

> *I am Sir Oracle and when I ope my mouth*
> *Let no man speak.*

10. *If you feel strongly about the way education is going, say so. If*

I have one regret it is this: when rubbish was being spoken, I did not punch hard enough. It does not matter what people call you, speak. For the last ten years I was doing the job, every aim, every examination, every component, every aspect and assumption was questioned, redefined, and, worst of all, swamped in a dreadful new language. In London and around the south-east I spent – no, I wasted – hundreds of hours listening to clones in grey suits telling me the latest decisions in the latest jargon. Blink and it changed. Blink, but you've moved the goal-posts. Blink, what goal-posts? New targets, new tiers, new criteria, new marks out of 60 not 100, no, that was last year, it's now 70, not 60, and if you don't mark like this, if you don't double-check everything against the criteria, you'll be penalising your candidates. But. No buts. But I can't understand the criteria, they're gobbledygook. Look, just do it. OK?

How much energy does a full-time teacher have to fight rubbish? Looking back, I feel exactly as Guildenstern does at the end of Stoppard's play: 'There must have been a moment, at the beginning, where we could have said – no. But somehow we missed it.' Instead, I ran backwards and forwards all through my forties, up to meetings, back to the department with new models, new cascade charts; I was a packhorse carrying bags full of brochures, courses, explanations, changes (what did it all cost?), and I sat up late into the night decoding it into simple English so that I could lead my department forward. Any good professional, I said to myself, is flexible and forward-looking. Adapt, Jonathan. Lead.

Right, OK, so this is what it means, I've got it now, and we can do it, honestly we can. Let's give it a go. Right? Good. On we go then. And on we went. But why would senior or 'top' teachers want to find the subject ever harder to administer while the substance of the courses became ever softer? Who wants to spend his life doing that? This protracted upheaval shortened some worthwhile careers and broke many HoDs, first by dissipating their energy, then by making their lives a misery.

Towards the end of my time as a head of department, a young and now very successful colleague told me that I was 'reactive rather than proactive'. Though I find that kind of language tedious I took the point. If true, it was time to go. Even if it wasn't true, at least I no longer had to go on saying things I did not believe. So, taking Edgar's words from the final speech of *King Lear*, I would urge all heads of department to

Speak what we feel, not what we ought to say.

33
God Save The Head

'May God forgive Warre!' A. C. Benson wrote of his Eton headmaster, Edmund Warre, 'I cannot.'

Over the last forty years I have heard so many similar remarks in schools, in gossipy, brutal, depressed, frustrated, acrimonious, splenetic, intriguing, alcoholic evenings around the dinner table or in the pub. Sooner or later, and usually sooner, the chat gets round to the head, and out come the machetes. By closing or stumbling-home time it's not so much a matter of 'May God forgive the head' as 'God help him!'

It's the same the world over, I suspect, in all schools, maintained and independent, and has been so in every age. Take the 1890s: 'That desperate man . . . Wretched Masters' Meeting. Warre's speech entirely devoid of courage, shrewdness, counsel or help.' What might a modern Benson confide in his diary a hundred years later?

What a terrible morning. Common-Room meeting. All target setting, statistics, league tables and Health and Safety. No vision and no discussion of any pupils. Considered throwing a brick through the head's window afterwards but remembered just in time the closed-circuit

TV cameras. The bursar spends his evenings scanning
these frame by frame. One can no longer safely urinate in
the grounds at midnight.

On leaving schoolmastering for the life of a don at Cambridge,
Benson reckoned he had spent three thousand hours on the
deadening work of writing out model classical verses, a soul-
destroying exercise that made him so angry *he* wanted to
throw a stone through the head's window. I have spent as
many hours – no, many more – head-watching, listening to
them at meetings, on committees, around playing fields, at
evening functions and in private, although not (I'm glad to
say) from the pulpit.

As close family members I had two heads (my father and
father-in-law, both in the state sector) and I have worked for
six heads, or nine if an interregnum counts as a headship and
if you include my times in Australia. I say I have worked for
these heads, though I am not sure whether 'for' is always the
right preposition. Well, certainly not against them, but with
varying degrees of enthusiasm.

As an assistant master . . . as a teacher (I cannot settle on
one or the other, so I'll keep alternating), as an assistant
master you work for a head and for the school if you feel that
you, the head and the school are pulling in the same direction.
It's a great feeling, a daily encouragement, and this direction
does not have to be grandly articulated into a vision statement
(about which I am sceptical) because it can be understood. If
the head, the staff and the pupils all feel that they are, broadly
speaking, in the same boat, you are in a happy school. As a
teacher you feel you are setting the pace and yet, paradoxically, you are being led.

In this collaborative atmosphere the creative energy flows
and that energy is transferred to the pupils. Teachers then run
the extra mile, teachers then live in good will, and this good

will encourages individuality and risk-taking and – a sign of a healthy community – can handle dissenting voices. It is important to respect and, if possible, to like the person you work for.

If you don't have that 'for' atmosphere in your teaching life you either become a bitter, disaffected bore or a professional knife-sharpener. Or, you can take the route I recommend: if, as a teacher, you feel undervalued by your head or disenchanted with the way you are being handled, you focus as clearly as you can on your pupils, on each lesson, on your primary function. Instead of eating yourself away, you say to yourself, 'It is not important whether or not I am not working for the head. I am working for the school, and for my pupils. That is why I am here.'

You escape from your professional stress into the classroom (passing on the way those ambitious teachers who cannot wait to escape from the classroom), because it is your pupils who matter. A good lesson makes you feel better, and a good lesson is so much more rewarding than Common-Room manoeuvres and staff intrigues. In other words, a head is not a school, though some heads behave as if they are. Critical of heads though I am and have been, when things are bad, when the boat seems to be the play thing of every wind, I concentrate more and more on my teaching. An irony, of course, because that is exactly what the head with whom you do not get on wants you to do.

My heads, in their very different ways, have all been very able and all had impressive qualities. My professional life has been mostly happy. These happy phases (during which I do not walk around grinning all the time) are characterised by there being few factions, a lively social life, and a generosity of spirit. You feel a sense of widespread mutual respect and notice a natural communal pride in what is being achieved.

At the risk of seeming sentimental, let me list some

personal actions for which I have been grateful to my heads. Add these together and you form an outline picture of a good head's – or, come to that, any good managing director's – human qualities:

(i) for being understanding when I had a disappointing set of results, the results coming on top of a professional and personal crisis in the department;

(ii) for dropping into the English Department and saying the place felt 'right', for pointing out that not one of the posters or photographs on the stairs was damaged or defaced, and that there was an attitude of warm respect in the building;

(iii) for coming along to play rehearsals when I was almost murderous or suicidal with stress, sitting quietly next to me, saying kind things and then coming along to the pub afterwards. And all that at the end of a day in which he had worked harder than I had;

(iv) for encouraging me to go on exchange, to take a sabbatical, and to write;

(v) for knowing in some detail about my family, and for asking about them;

(vi) for telling me some of his problems;

(vii) for giving me a packet of Maltesers each time I mentioned Tonbridge in radio interviews;

(viii) for telling me that – far from taking me away from school – my writing and lecturing helped the school and its wider reputation;

(ix) for ringing me up when we had been unnecessarily sharp with each other in public, and saying that was fine, we could both handle it;

(x) for making me laugh and – this is crucially important – for laughing at my comments. I can't stand those plonkers who stare at you stony-faced after you've said something funny. Humourless heads, in my opinion, need a good shoe-ing.

Perhaps all the points listed above could be explained away

as charming insincerity. Insincerity? Guff? Diplomacy? Massaging Jonathan's ego? Call it any of those if you like, but the fact that I can so easily remember those moments, indeed that I unashamedly treasure them, suggests that they were personally and – if you want to be Machiavellian – professionally effective. Because they kept me going, and made me work harder. Working for the head, if you like, but as a result of that for the school, for my pupils, and all done willingly and with a sense of great personal satisfaction.

If teaching has never been more demanding than it is now – if I am right in that – then the need for professional warmth and encouragement is ever more necessary. This applies to the teacher in his last years just as much as the teacher in his first terms or in middle career. All teachers need encouragement. All heads need encouragement.

It is not possible for heads always to encourage, sympathise and support. There are only so many hours in a day, and they themselves are under unrelenting pressure. Sometimes heads have understandably run out of patience and their support is no longer earned; sometimes teachers simply do not deserve any more propping up, let alone warrant any more indulgence. But in a performing, creative, adrenalin-sapping job like ours encouragement remains the best incentive. Why else are actors always hugging each other and telling each other they are wonderful? Teachers are actors too.

Shaun MacLaughlin, who produced all my radio plays, tells the story of a radio producer who had badly miscast a part. Head in hands, he sat alone in his studio listening to the rehearsal tape. It was a terrible take. They'd have to do it again and again. The actor was downstairs. What could he say? What on earth could he do? Suddenly he stood up, bounced down to the recording room and spoke directly to the actor. 'Well done, my dear, well done! And now, let's . . . *build* on it.'

Every one of the heads I have worked for, with or under has been harshly criticised, some consistently, some occasionally. If they – if you – heard all that was being said behind their backs would they jump under a bus? No, because (a) they know it is all being said behind their backs because they themselves said it behind the backs of the heads they worked for, with and under. Indeed future heads (an easy species to spot) are often the most devastating critics in any school, clearing the undergrowth in a sharp cutting action which suggests that the broom metaphor will be out of date in the new millennium. And they won't jump under a bus because (b) they sent in an application form for the head's job, didn't they, and in many cases went on sending in application forms until they were successful, until the three lemons came up in a row, until the five lottery balls plus the bonus number all rolled out, until the answers they were giving were the answers the appointing governors wanted to hear.

And, anyway, you don't *have* to be a headmaster, do you? No one begged you to put on your helmet, grill, arm guard, abdominal protector, chest guard, leg pads, thigh pads, inner thigh pad and go out there to face the bouncers and the throat balls, did they? You could instead sit safely among the crowd and criticise from a distance, and mock the incompetent ones ducking and weaving in the firing line – even enjoy seeing a bit of blood being spilt. After all, although it remains the convention for most schools to have a head, you don't have to be one.

I have been a head twice, on both occasions for one evening only, and I have to say one evening was enough. The day you are appointed a head is, I am told by my headmaster friends, the best day of your headship, and I have taken them at their word.

On the two evenings I was a head (in 1970 and 1975) I was cast for the role by my colleagues as we gave farewell parties and revues to two leaving heads. In truth, I was promoted to the hot seat and handed the mortar board not because I have all the necessary qualities (charisma, high-mindedness, determination, decisiveness, a thick skin and a financial grip) but because I am 6 feet 2 inches tall, a brilliant height for any aspiring head. Indeed for many years 6 feet 2 inches was a prerequisite for the ultimate promotion, though I have recently noticed that an alarming number of middle-sized, even small, people are now getting the nod. I also had (then) dark hair with just enough grey at the temples to suggest a steadily deepening gravitas. Furthermore I had a bit of acting ability, or at least a talent for taking off tones of voice and catching those give-away movements in body language, those unconscious leakages of a head's suppressed but real motives.

(But if I could act the part for a night, the devil tempted me, why not act it for the rest of my career, why not do it for good? Think of the power. Think of the way people would hang on your every decision. Think of the honour and of the wealth, Faustus! . . . No, no, Faustus, these are illusions and the fruits of lunacy, think of the *life*!)

One brief sketch I wrote in 1970 about Michael McCrum, who was leaving Tonbridge to become head of Eton, went as follows (with the stage directions in brackets):

(In academic dress, dark suit and mortar board, exuding the aforementioned gravitas and iron self-control, I – for the moment Michael McCrum – sit at my huge study desk writing one of my crisp memos, a memo designed to give whoever picks it out of his pigeonhole an apoplectic fit. The door is knocked. This, by the way, was in the days when you could still see a head without waiting a fortnight and then going through a security cordon of secretaries and senior staff. Hearing the knock, the head

does not look up. Not looking up, of course, confers
higher status. The head speaks in a slightly world-weary
way.)
HEAD: Come.
(Peter, a keen young teacher, enters.)
HEAD (not looking up):Yes, Peter, do sit down.
(Peter sits in the chair. There is only one chair, which has
a seat which goes slowly down as he sits, like a slowly
deflating balloon. You can almost hear the slow deflation
in the seat and in Peter. Within a minute, with the head
still absorbed in his crisp despatch of business, Peter is
practically prostrate on his back. After taking his time to
blow the ink dry, the head stands and goes to the drinks
tray.)
HEAD: Sherry, Peter?
PETER: Thank you, Headmaster.
(There are two glasses. The head fills a large tumbler
brimful of sherry and hands it down to Peter. He pours a
thimbleful glass for himself. He opens up a step-ladder,
checks it is steady, climbs it, sits on the top step with his
knees together and smiles.)
HEAD: Right, Peter, what exactly is your problem?

As a sketch, it has some affinity with an incident at Loretto
School in 1964. A senior housemaster had had enough (a
familiar scene), more than enough (a familiar scene), of seeing
the school being turned into something he did not like.
(Heads, in the view of many senior housemasters, are prone to
do this.) Anyway, the dialogue this time was as brief as in the
first story but the meeting was all over much more quickly.

(The housemaster marches over to the head's study,
knocks, walks in without waiting for a response, and
walks towards the startled head.)

HOUSEMASTER: Headmaster, I'd be very grateful if you would make a decision!
HEADMASTER: Yes, of course, Chris, what about?
HOUSEMASTER: Anything, Headmaster, anything.

It is, of course, easy to list all the qualities you hope to find in a head. Obviously you cannot do the job without mental and physical resilience, without a grasp of detail, and without a sense of priorities. To those I would add the ability to inspire (how can you lead a school without this?), optimism (because I'm something of a pessimist myself) and the ability to distinguish between those on the staff who are worth listening to and those who are not, and clearly we would all expect to fall into the first category. I certainly would. That brings in perception, judgement and good gut instincts.

Equally I can imagine school governors, in their hard-boiled way, laughing at my half-baked list, and drawing up a rather different profile: a grasp of economic realities, good with parents, ruthlessness, skilful at promoting and selling the school, a person determined to move the school up the league tables, a person not afraid to cut out the dead wood (to fire with enthusiasm), a person to take the school into the next millennium . . . That sort of chat. I once described a head with all the characteristics I did not like and a school governor said to me, 'That's exactly the sort of person we're after.'

In 1990, Shaun MacLaughlin asked me if I would develop an idea for a four-play serial for BBC Radio. That summer in France I came up with *The Head Man*, which turned into two series, eight plays in all. I did not want to write a schooly series with lots of classroom conflicts and cabbagey corridors and smoking in the bike sheds and bullying in the lavatories, but to focus instead on the fascinating professional adult world of a school: the politics, the struggles and stresses involved at the top in education, the public stances and the embattled private lives of the head, his family and his close-knit team.

After reading my first set of plays, the Head of Radio Drama shook his head ruefully and said to me:

'My God, it's just like the BBC!'

Whether that is a compliment to the teaching profession or not, it does suggest that such pressures – be they on Director Generals or heads or airline pilots – are comparable. What might seem to some a dull topic, the headship of a very academic school, to me seems full of dramatic potential. I saw an opportunity to explore the head's relationships with his staff, his wife, his children, his publisher and his lover. I wanted to make the listener feel the tension between his loss of idealism and his burning ambition, to understand a man torn between his assured public/media persona and his confessional inner voice: such conflicts are captured more convincingly and felt more deeply on radio than in any other medium. Furthermore, the head's wife has a senior role at the local comprehensive, and this enabled me to dramatise a philosophical and political ambivalence at the core of my own position.

Patrick Balfour, my hero, was a talented, flawed man, and a man much more able and much more interesting to me than those who daily took him to the cleaners behind his back. He was not based (laugh, if you like) on any head I knew, nor was he an amalgam. He became real for me, with a life of his own, and his presence still shadows me. I often feel in his shoes, and feel uncomfortable in them. With Patrick Balfour, rather as at those farewell revues, I was able to be a head and not to be a head, to imagine being a head but to wake up being myself. Give me fiction any time.

When the series came out, and even more when the plays were repeated, I had a huge mail bag. (Well, huge for me.) Letters came in from all over the country, from state schools and from the independent sector, from heads and teachers and secretaries and parents, but mostly from those inside the profession, nearly all asking me if I had ever taught in their school or (cunning) did I perhaps have a friend/mole at their school who had blown the gaff on their head and the senior staff. Five letters accused me of writing specifically about five different heads (they named them), none of whom I had ever met or more than vaguely heard of. One was delighted that I had exposed his head for all the dreadful things he had done but had not yet been caught for. 'You've fixed the bastard!' he said. 'You've really fixed him!'

'The trouble is,' some wrote, 'I can't tell whether I like him or not, or whether you want me to like him or not.'

Well, quite!

Even so, as a classroom teacher well down the final furlong, I still enjoy watching this or that young colleague making his way. He is not difficult to pick out. He arrives and is high on public visibility. He tells everyone all he does. He takes every opportunity to speak in public. He is pointed out. After a couple of terms he asks if he can be promoted to second in the department. Number Two in the department! Good heavens, he's only just arrived. And after a couple more years at the most – he doesn't want to get bogged down – he applies for, and gets, a department. It is amazing. Running a department. Or a house? *That* person! And in no time he's applying for a deputy headship. *In*-credible. Would you believe it? And he gets one. He gets one! From there it is only a short step – and spraying a few application forms – to a headship. And, yes, he actually becomes a head. You can't believe it. You're in a daze. You pinch yourself. And after a few years at most as a head – he does not want to become bogged down – after he's mucked that school up, he applies for another headship. He plans to move on to a Big school. In-cred-i-ble! And he gets it. It's in the papers!

Between thirty-five and fifty I was sometimes asked by

those who mistake height for ballast if I wanted to be a head. I always said no and I always meant it. I suspect I was suspected of not telling the truth, of deceitful diffidence or of playing a canny game. My father thought I would be a head. I told him I wouldn't. 'Wait till you see the others,' he would say. I know what he meant, oh I do know what he meant, but even that didn't sharpen the spur. I'd rather watch other people do it: I'd rather watch a Woody Allen film than be Woody Allen.

Though I have lived from my earliest days with heads (my father was, you remember, appointed when I was seven) I have never applied for such a post, though I have been asked to – but, good God, who *hasn't*! Perhaps I could have done parts of it but not enough. It obviously didn't sufficiently matter to me – it didn't compel me – and wanting such a job, really wanting it, is critical. I also think I would have been less fulfilled if I had left the classroom. I do feel teaching is what I was meant to do. Yes, it's a great pity and a professional disgrace that the only way you can make decent money as a teacher is to stop teaching, but even the money a head earns is not temptation enough. That would be doing the right deed (or in my case the wrong deed) for the wrong reason.

If I had been a head I would have resented the loss of much of my private life. Many of the hours I spent playing with my children would not have been there. I would not have read as much. I would have written less. I'm not good on committees. I'm not good at telling people unpalatable truths. I'm hopeless with money. I quickly resent doing things I do not want to do, particularly in a formal social context. I might well have ended up barking.

My lack of Christian belief would also have ruled me out of most of the schools I might otherwise have considered. Although, over the years, I have to say, a few of my colleagues, when opening the *Times Educational Supplement* and running their eyes over the headships available, and finding that the applicants should be practising members of this or that church, have rediscovered their faith just in time to make the short list. Not so much a drama on the road to Damascus, then, as a quiet moment next to the tea trolley.

34

The Parent From Hell

Every school has a Parent From Hell. Unless you're very lucky it is usually more than one. Mention a difficult pupil's name and the teacher puts his hands over his face, 'No, listen, seriously, have you met his mother?' or, 'God, poor kid, what do you expect, you should meet his father!' or, the double whammy: 'Wait till you meet his *parents!*' (Was Philip Larkin right? I'll come back to that.)

So, since every school has its quota of Parents From Hell, when a parents' evening is coming up I tend to think, 'I could do without this.' At my school we have five parents' evenings a year. Coming on top of a full day's teaching this can be the last thing I want: I'm talked out already, linguistically dehydrated, and the evening lasts between three and four hours. Some schools go into theirs almost straight after the last lesson; ours begin at 6.45, so you usually haven't eaten properly and you daren't slam down a big Scotch because you'll be breathing booze all over them, and what kind of an example is that, eh, from an example-setting profession?

Yet at the end of every parents' evening I always feel 'I enjoyed that. Have I really seen over twenty sets of parents – and not one from hell?' As I walk home, my eye on *NYPD*

Blue and the seriously delayed Scotch, I feel I now understand some of my pupils in that year group better. By talking with the parents even for a brief time, swapping perceptions and concerns and planning encouraging strategies, I can (in the current slang) see where my pupils are coming from.

When I was a boy in Wales there were no parents' evenings. Apart from a passing word, if that, with the house-master at the beginning and end of term, my parents never met my teachers. When I started to teach in Scotland there were no parents' evenings. If any fool in the staff room ever suggested we should have them the usual response was 'Parents? Who the hell wants parents? What's it got to do with *them*? This is a private matter between the pupils and us. The next thing we'll have is the parents picking the teams.'

Then they started, first one examination year, then the two big examination years, until now when it is assumed you have a parents' evening for every year group in the school. It is so obviously right that it's hard to believe it was ever other-wise.

Even in boarding schools, the once absent parents are now increasingly present: at functions, at weekends, on the touch-line and on the boundary, on the telephone, at plays, asking questions, checking up: being parents, in fact. This has been a massive development over the last decade. The mothers in particular are now major players, so most schools, day and boarding, are not only asking themselves how the schools look and feel, they are playing the family card. In education every year has become The Year of The Family. At school we all play Happy Families now.

As a father I had the usual clashes at home with my chil-dren: they were coming in late, being rude, not making an effort, taking liberties, taking everything for granted, taking us for granted, comparing their parents unfavourably with better-off parents . . . all about as usual as you can get. I particularly disliked it when they had big rows between themselves; and I still do. I particularly disliked it when they were rude to their mother, and I still do.

Sometimes I completely lost my temper. As I do that very rarely it shook me and them to the core. Nothing upsets me more than family matters, and that goes for most people. Talking about family problems, talking through family rows – both within the family and with friends – has proved the best way to come to terms with what is happening. A father, a parent of three boys, once told me, 'However bad it gets, never cut off, never stop talking. My sons have done most things. Keep listening, that's what I do.' And listening usually achieves more than giving advice.

As a teacher you as often see overambitious and unrealistic parents asking too much of their children as you see self-satisfied parents asking too little. I teach a few boys who are clearly very tense all the time, prone to cry suddenly, and that can usually be traced – you don't have to be a rocket scientist to spot it – to a father who expects too much, who expects his son to get wonderful results in examinations, to be successful in sport, to obtain grade eight in his musical examinations and so forth. The father's eyes tell you he expects nothing else. Indeed at parents' evenings he tells you.

When I saw the film *Shine* lots of men and women stayed in their seats afterwards, upset, comforting each other, and some openly weeping. This was not the quick-easy-cry-and-dab-your-eyes that follows a bog-standard sentimental movie. This was an experience which had re-opened the pain of not living up to Daddy, of letting Daddy down. When you see *Death of a Salesman* exactly the same happens. Both are about fathers and sons, about excessive expectation, disillusionment and family breakdown. Both are about not facing up to the effect you have on your own children.

It's the same at the other end of the scale: underperforming pupils who find any reason to explain their lack of application and then solicit, and quickly receive, their parents' support in blaming their teachers and their school. There is no doubt that some teaching deserves criticism, and I am keen to address and analyse that issue, but I am here talking of another matter. Socially self-indulgent parents can be extraordinarily blind to their own part in their children's underperformance, parents who are so busily bound up with their own ambition, with making their own way and their own money, that they are never really there for their children – they just fit them in when they can. They tune in occasionally, usually at crisis points, and usually too late.

'I suppose all I can do is go on loving them?' parents often say, with a bruised but brave smile. A straightforward yes is called for and usually given, and yet that is usually too easy an answer. The right answer, which I never give face to face, is it depends what you mean by 'all' and it depends what you mean by 'loving'. 'Good parenting,' my daughter used to say with a laugh, once I had thrown up my hands and given in. It's the kind of mockery that hurts because you know you have taken the easy option.

At such times, I tend to say to myself, 'It's all very well Churchill saying "Never Give In", but that was war time, that was only a world war, that was on the beaches and the landing grounds, that was in the fields and in the streets, that's easy, I'd never surrender there, because I'd rather fight on the beaches or in the desert or in the Pacific than deal with my son in full flow or my daughter in her present mood. I'm giving in, if you're listening, God, because I can't take any more, I'm giving in because there's no fight left in me.' Or I may go for the tactical-retreat-but-I know-what-I'm-doing, 'Yes, I'm giving in *this* time, yes, I've lost this one, but I'm resolving here and now to fight another day. When I've got my strength back. Don't imagine for one moment that this is the end of the matter. No, this is not the end, it is not even the beginning of the end, but it is the end of the beginning.'

One thing is certain: in schools, parents are in. In the independent sector in particular, where the mothers are inspecting every room and the parents have the buying power, the generic term 'Parents' is now quoted endlessly by heads. Far from being irrelevant, in these pupil-poaching days parents are The Big Issue. Parents are what it's all about. 'It won't go down well with the parents,' we're told. 'Parents expect nothing less,' we're told. 'Tell that to the parents,' comes the sharp reply. 'Our parents won't stand for it.' 'The parents are beginning to mutter.' 'It's vital on this one that we get the parents back on our side.' 'Rightly or wrongly, parents still have this perception of us as a . . .' 'I'm happy to report that the parents are very pleased when they look around and see . . .' 'The word among the parents is . . .'

The body politic, it now seems, is the parental body (which includes, of course, the parents from hell), that mixture of dinner party circuit, Chinese whispers, secret police, inside track and Deep Throat. Independent schools rise and fall on what the parents think. When a head is found *in flagrante* or with a bottom drawer full of porn or is being sacked for something else, parents form unofficial and opposing action groups. Parents, we are told, are up in arms and about to vote with their feet. Parental cash, as never before, is at the root of all this, and in a business climate how could it be otherwise? The corridors of power in the independent sector now have their ears tuned in to the Parents' Line. And the lines are open twenty-four hours a day.

When a head wants to bring in an unpopular idea (unpopular with his staff and pupils, I mean) or to make a change he has been secretly planning for years and has finally drummed up the courage to break, he'll usually say, 'Parents always tell me this is what they want', or 'This is the first thing parents always say when I have an interview.' One famous head of my acquaintance used this Mythical Parent ploy once too often. He was standing up, outlining his latest plan, and finished with his supporting and well-researched justification:

'And, above all, parents are adamant about it.'

Suddenly a confident voice came from the back of the room, the voice of a senior housemaster with only two years to go and nothing to fear:

'Names, please, Headmaster. Names of the adamant parents.'

Nice.

As a teacher, parents can be for or against you. Whether you have that support or not is not always important but it can be critical. My father, as you know, came from the Rhondda Valley and first taught there. (No, please, not another *How Green Was My Valley* anecdote.) He'd had trouble with a wild boy. He firmly disciplined him. First thing the next morning, glancing away from the sums on his blackboard, something caught his eye out of the classroom window. The boy's father was coming across the playground. The man was still in his pit clothes, his face grimed with coal dust, straight from the night shift. He'd been home, heard from his wife about his son's punishment, and set out straightaway for school before changing. He knocked on my father's door.

'Mr Smith,' he said, 'is Gwyn here?'

My father pointed out the boy in the third row.

'Come here, Gwyn.'

The miner got hold of the boy, took him outside and gave him a hiding. He pushed the boy back in the classroom door.

'Sorry, Mr Smith. We're all sorry.'

By the end of his career, forty years later, my father said that would not have happened. Not that he wanted the boy beaten or bullied. Most certainly he did not; most certainly I do not. Neither of us used or believed in corporal punishment. His point was that by the late 1960s, when he retired, the teacher had become the target for abuse from parents. That parent would have been coming across the yard to remonstrate with my father. Any misbehaviour had become the teacher's fault: either he couldn't keep control or he was out of touch or he was picking on this boy or girl. The child was now in the right. Respect for the teacher was fast diminishing.

My teaching world is different, easier on one level, more subtle and more sniping on another. I face different kinds of parental request and more oblique kinds of criticism. If a pupil is going through a particularly stroppy patch (sometimes called the tunnel), parents might well ask the teacher (face to face or on the telephone) to help them to 'sort him out, to have a word with him, he'll listen to you, he won't listen to us, he's become so rude, that's when he even bothers to speak at all, but if it comes from you he might take it. Would you, please, at least try, it can't do any harm. We'd be most grateful.'

Teachers, surprise surprise, like this. It's not that they're agony aunts or think they know the answers; it's that to help in this way is one of the reasons they're in the job. The word I have with the stroppy student doesn't always work, but if I'm asked by a parent to see what I can do I'll spend hours on it. Those on the pastoral side of the school (all teachers, one hopes), certainly housemasters and tutors and heads of year, spend much of their year doing exactly this. All teachers like to help someone round a corner or through the tunnel, and going through adolescence can feel full of corners and tunnels.

There is a spell between thirteen and eighteen, give or take a year, when even the most charitable child suspects his parent might be the Parent From Hell, when whatever your parents say to you or ask you to do is stupid or boring or pointless or cringey or hypocritical or bloody obvious or at the very least something they've rabbited on about a million times before. Even at their best parents are pretty embarrassing. You don't even know where to look. I even remember being embarrassed about how embarrassing I found them, as well as being unsure whether to kiss my mother in public. Looking round first to see if anyone was watching was also fairly embarrassing, a grim but guilty tactic.

I remember, too, when I stopped kissing my father and started to shake hands with him. The idea, I suppose, was that I was now grown up and more manly and young manly chaps did not kiss their fathers. I wish I had gone on kissing him, and I am glad my children have done so with me. Either way, at whatever point the young cross the shadow-line and the green sickness of late youth descends, whatever the problems between you and however long it goes on, by their early twenties most children seem to have moved back towards their parents.

The criticisms I take (on parents' evenings) are often coded. I'll give you some examples and then translate them into blunt English, or give you the reply I would dearly love to make. One day I'll say them all. (Becky: Oh, *yes*, Dad, I'm sure you will. Like you always do!)

1. Parent (looking at partner): But he used to be so good at his English, darling, didn't he?
   Translation: You're a crap teacher, Mr Smith.

2. Parent (looking at partner): At his last school he loved his English, darling, didn't he? Absolutely loved it. And when he was little his English teacher – what *was* her name, she was always so encouraging – was always putting his poems and stories on the wall, he was so excited and happy about that, wasn't he, darling, you couldn't stop him talking and writing, and she used to do little plays and things, and he was always in them.
   Translation: You're a crap teacher, Mr Smith.

3. Parent: There obviously seems to be a personality clash somewhere.

   Unspoken reply: No, there isn't. There is no personality clash. What there is is this. Your son is being unpleasant and doing no work. I am not accepting your unpleasant son's unpleasant behaviour. I am also not accepting fifty-fifty responsibility on this. He's the problem, though I am beginning to think that it just might be you . . .

4. Parent (straight from the pub): So, everything's going well then, good-good, he's happy, and everything's fine?

   Unspoken reply: Good God, he hasn't told you *that*, has he!

5. Parent: I can't think why he doesn't read, darling, can you?

   Unspoken reply: Oh, I think I can.

6. Mother: Of course, he's got such a brilliant sister. It's very difficult for him.

   Unspoken reply: God, spare me this one, just this one, God, and I'll forgive you all the other cock-ups. Just because he's got a vocabulary of ninety-three words (on a good day) really should not be blamed on his brilliant sister. But The Brilliant Sister problem is seriously on the increase in Kent and the south-east. The Kent and South-East Health Authority should immediately release some NHS funding to deal with this syndrome, this virus which is decimating male confidence. It's worse than spots. Spots go away. Sisters, infamously, do not. In fact many of the pupils I teach now have a brilliant sister who by her very brilliance has made life quite simply unsupportable for the poor lad I'm teaching. In fact I'm beginning to feel a bit of male bonding coming on here. In fact I'm beginning to look forward to the next lesson and to telling the lads that I'm all with them, with them all the way, when it comes to hating the brilliant sister sitting upstairs with her head stuck into a book, a big book, her back to the radiator and her nose in Charlotte Brontë and Jane Austen and George Eliot (oh, yes, George was a woman too) and Virginia Woolf and Sylvia Plath and Margaret Drabble and A. S. Byatt, and all that lot were brilliant sisters I bet, while my poor lads are being normal and watching *Match of the Day* and *Men Behaving Badly*. Hell's teeth, it's bad enough being a boy going round corners and in and out of tunnels without being the younger brother of A Brilliant Sister.

Then there are the full-on parental rows between father and mother happening right before your eyes. These I do love. You can sit back, take a break, and watch it all unfold.

FATHER (looking at teacher, not at wife): Well, that's what *she* thinks.

MOTHER (looking at husband, not at teacher): So, what do *you* think?

FATHER: Doesn't matter what I think, does it, it's all about you and him, isn't it? It always is.

MOTHER: No, what I'm asking is, why don't you ever give him any support? Whenever anything goes wrong, you want to know. Always. You only want to know when everything is going wrong. Not when he does anything good.

FATHER: Why don't you listen to Mr Smith? We've come here to hear what he has to say. The whole world knows what you think.

MOTHER: You can't even get here on time, you don't even know what subjects he's taking.

Generally speaking, the mother does know far more about the child than the father does. They're better informed. They know more about a child's world. They have listened more over the years. They are also more persistent in their questioning, and none more so than the mothers who are teachers. It comes out, however hard they try to hide it, oh, yes, it comes out.

Most dads behave as if they're at the doctor's or the dentist's. They can take it but they'd rather be anywhere else. They can't quite bring themselves to admit they have got a problem, and they'll be glad when it's all over and they can get out. They look immensely relieved at the end of the last interview.

One of the silliest encounters I have had (I've had this one a few times) goes as follows:

FATHER: So, how's it going, Mr Smith?

ME: Very well, he's doing excellently.

MOTHER: Is he!

ME: He certainly is.

MOTHER: Gosh, this is a surprise, isn't it, dear?

FATHER: Not really.

MOTHER: Mr Smith says he's doing very well.

FATHER: I know, I heard.

MOTHER: And it's never been his strong subject. This is *so* encouraging!

ME: I don't know why you say it isn't his strong subject. He's fluent, thoughtful, he writes well and he talks well.

MOTHER: Talks well? This is wonderful, usually he just glares at me, last holidays he was so withdrawn, not a squeak, well, apart from his music.

ME: So, he's turned the corner, that's great. Not that he's ever been anything but helpful with me.

FATHER: So Mark's going to get an A? Good.

ME: Mark? I thought we were talking about Andrew?

MOTHER: Andrew? No, it's Mark.

FATHER: Don't tell me we're talking to the wrong teacher?

MOTHER: It *is* the geography Mr Smith, isn't it?

ME: No, I'm the English Mr Smith. Geography Mr Smith is the nice-looking young one upstairs.

FATHER (to wife): You might at least write their names down properly!

That's all more fun than the mother who came in, eyed me directly and declaimed four nicely turned sentences. Not a spare word. Usually there is a marked difference between how people speak and how they write (though it is a difference which is blurring day by day) and this woman spoke as if she were writing. I was a little taken aback.

'Yes?' I said.

'That,' she said with a venomous sting, 'is what you wrote about my son.'

'Oh,' I said, 'I'm sure I didn't. It's not the sort of thing I write.'

'Oh yes you did!'

And she took out of her handbag the previous term's report, pressed open on the first page. It was what I had written. She had learnt it off by heart.

'Well,' I said, 'it depends how you say it.'

'Really?'

'Absolutely.'

'You read it out then.'

But even with the warmest tone I could find it still didn't quite catch fire. Most parents, though, do want to hear something close to the truth, preferably the near-truth kindly put, and topped and tailed with encouragement. If you want to, you can get away with bland charm all evening but that's no good.

If you're feeling on very skilful form you can try the 'Oxford sandwich'. The Oxford sandwich is the technique of putting the only important bit in the middle, with a nice wedge of bread and butter on either side, e.g. 'Lovely man, no mind of course, gorgeous wife.' Or, 'He's a nice boy, not a great listener, works really hard.' This presupposes, of course, that the message is understood. It's a dangerous game. With most parents you do have to be very careful and I have found even the mildest qualification can be taken out of context and used against you.

Some teachers have no time for such niceties. They can be quite extraordinarily blunt. One physics teacher, with no social preliminaries, said to a parent: 'Your son is doing badly. He's doing no work. He's going to fail.' And that was my wife's first interview that evening. Fortunately I was on duty as a teacher elsewhere in the building so did not, as a father, have to hear my son's performance in physics so succinctly put. Fortunately, too, things got better as the evening wore on.

As a father I did not enjoy my daughter's parents' evenings, partly because I went along defensively, and partly because I went along as an undercover teacher.

'Why don't you say something?' my wife would say as we walked from one interview to another.

'They'll only spot I'm a teacher. They can spot it a mile off.'

'What does that matter?'

'Teachers hate talking to parents who are teachers.'

'No, *you* hate it. I'm a teacher and they're talking to me.'

But I still said very little, apart from too many thank yous and conveying a general sense of grovelling gratitude.

You should, of course, be able to talk about all your pupils to their parents without finding it necessary to look at your mark book. Few things are more dispiriting for a parent than to sit and watch while a teacher runs a ruler down a class list in his mark book, then watch him run his eye along the ruler's edge to see how the pupil is getting on. What a buoyant human experience that is! If his pupils have made that little impression on him he'd be better looking for a job in another field.

The best approach is to be friendly and direct. Stress the good things and suggest one area in which, as parents and teachers, you can work together to improve the child's performance. That's likely to be in attitude and in confidence. Don't say too much. I find if I go on talking I tie myself into elaborate, overqualifying tangles, with saving clauses, on the one hand and on the other, and a touch of soft soap. All the good work is undone. The first three or four sentences can say it all. Even if they sit staring at you, try not to unpick it.

35
The Shadow-Line

The opening section of *The Shadow-Line* by Joseph Conrad.

Only the young have such moments. I don't mean the very young. No. The very young have, properly speaking, no moments. It is the privilege of early youth to live in advance of its days in all the beautiful continuity of hope which knows no pauses and no introspection.

One closes behind one the little gate of mere boyishness – and enters an enchanted garden. Its very shades glow with promise. Every turn of its path has its seduction. And it isn't because it is an undiscovered country. One knows well enough that all mankind had streamed that way. It is the charm of universal experience from which one expects an uncommon or personal sensation – a bit of one's own.

One goes on recognising the landmarks of the predecessors, excited, amused, taking the hard luck and the good luck together – the kicks and the halfpence, as the saying is – the picturesque common lot that holds so many possibilities for the deserving or perhaps for the lucky. Yes. One goes on. And the time, too, goes on – till one perceives ahead a shadow-line warning one that the region of early youth, too, must be left behind.

This is the period of life in which such moments of which I have spoken are likely to come. What moments? Why, the moments of boredom, of weariness, of dissatisfaction. Rash moments. I mean moments when the still young are inclined to commit rash actions, such as getting married suddenly or else throwing up a job for no reason.

This is not a marriage story. It wasn't so bad as that with me. My action, rash as it was, had more the character of divorce – almost of desertion. For no reason on which a sensible person could put a finger I threw up my job – chucked my berth – left the ship of which the worst that could be said was that she was a steamship and therefore, perhaps, not entitled to that blind loyalty which . . . However, it's no use trying to put a gloss on what even at the time I myself half suspected to be a caprice.

It was in an Eastern port. She was an Eastern ship, inasmuch as then she belonged to that port. She traded among dark islands on a blue reef-scarred sea . . . a most excellent Scottish ship – for she was that from the keel up – excellent sea-boat, easy to keep clean, most handy in every way, and if it had not been for her internal propulsion, worthy of any man's love. I cherish to this day a profound respect for her memory. As to the kind of trade she was engaged in and the character of my ship-mates, I could not have been happier if I had had the life and the men made to my order by a benevolent Enchanter.

And suddenly I left all this. I left it in that, to us, inconsequential manner in which a bird flies away from a comfortable branch. It was as though all unknowing I had heard a whisper or seen something. Well – perhaps! One day I was perfectly right and the next everything was

gone – glamour, flavour, interest, contentment – everything. It was one of those moments, you know. The green
sickness of late youth descended on me and carried me
off. Carried me off that ship, I mean.

The Captain stared hard as if wondering what ailed
me. But he was a sailor, and he, too, had been young at
one time. Presently a smile came to lurk under his thick
iron-grey moustache, and he observed that, of course, if I
felt I must go he couldn't keep me by main force. And it
was arranged that I should be paid off the next morning.
As I was going out of the chart-room he added suddenly,
in a peculiar wistful tone, that he hoped I would find
what I was so anxious to go and look for. A soft, cryptic
utterance which seemed to reach deeper than any
diamond-hard tool could have done. I do believe he
understood my case.

36
That Poem

Thinking of parental influence and the green sickness of late youth, *that poem* keeps coming back to me. Try as I might I can't help it. It just stays there, stubbornly, memorably, going round and round in my head. Other people admit it's the same with them. Like it or lump it, love it or hate it, they can all quote the ruddy thing. There are so many other poems about families and the generations, and sons and fathers and daughters and mothers – school anthologies are full of them – but that's the one we can all reel off.

In 1974, when I was teaching in Melbourne, my parents-in-law brought me out from England the new Philip Larkin collection, *High Windows*. I can still feel the shock and exhilaration as I read through those poems for the first time. It was the most arresting new book I had opened since Tom Stoppard's *Rosencrantz and Guildenstern Are Dead* in 1967. Speaking of the collection Larkin said, 'There are some quite nasty ones in it,' and certainly some of the language struck me, on that first reading, as brutal. Certainly, too, there was a defiant denial, an aggressive disgust with sex and a consuming fear of death.

Yet I understood his fears and sympathised with his defensiveness over life's unfulfilled desires. He spoke to me. I also saw in the poems a new celebration of the seasons, a new reaching out, and an awareness of the potential for other people to have undiminished lives. It was also, as so often with Larkin, bleakly funny, a humour of a perfectly serious sort, the sort of humour a number of my close friends have. The poems gave me immense pleasure, scoring highly on the nod factor (nodding at the truth of his perceptions of the human condition . . . that's mainly what I read for, the nod factor).

I had become a father only a few months earlier and was, as is natural, a besotted dad. In that long Australian summer I sat by my daughter's cot for hours. How would life treat her? How amazing that I should now have a child, that I should soon be called Daddy. The only Daddy I knew was my father. The generations roll on. Every parent knows that feeling, those hours full of pride, anxiety, hope and wonder. So to sit there, by her cot, reading Larkin's famous/infamous poem about parents and children and the generations was disturbing. Although they are probably the best-known and the most T-shirt-quoted lines of poetry written in the last thirty years, I want, if you will bear with me, to look at them again:

THIS BE THE VERSE

They fuck you up, your mum and dad,
  They may not mean to, but they do.
They fill you with the faults they had,
  And add some extra, just for you.

But they were fucked up in their turn
  By fools in old-style hats and coats,
Who half the time were soppy-stern
  And half at one another's throats.

Man hands on misery to man
  It deepens like a coastal shelf.

> *Get out as early as you can,*
> *And don't have any kids yourself.*

When discussing this poem it is customary for readers to go straight to that first, shocking, arresting line. How can you say that of your parents? What a disgusting remark! It is far more instructive instead to look first at the unusual title Larkin chooses, and to explore the background it betokens. What on earth can it mean? What is it doing there? It is taken, of course, from Robert Louis Stevenson's poem 'Requiem', the last verse of which is also the epitaph engraved on Stevenson's tomb in Samoa:

> *Under the wide and starry sky*
> *Dig the grave and let me lie.*
> *Glad did I live and gladly die,*
> *And I laid me down with a will.*

> *This be the verse you grave for me:*
> Here he lies where he longed to be;
> Home is the sailor, home from sea,
> And the hunter home from the hill.

Given that Larkin's poem is clearly about parents and children, what was Stevenson's relationship with his father? After all, titles are a very important part of any poem, and Larkin's is surely directing us to look up Stevenson's life. What was Robert Louis's view of his father? And what hopes did Stevenson's father have for his son, his sickly, 'chesty' only child. Very straightforward hopes, in fact. His engineer father hoped and expected his son would follow him – and be an engineer. His son would, in due course, join him in the profession and become a Victorian gentleman.

Things with families, particularly with creative families, are rarely so easy. Though meant by his father to be an engineer, R.L.S. trained instead as a lawyer before reacting fully against his father's wishes and against the overwhelming Calvinism of his Edinburgh upbringing. No old-style hats and coats for him. He went the whole bohemian hog: he wore velvet. He also stopped going to church – no light decision in that time and in that Edinburgh household – and from that day on his father never whistled again.

Then, as soon as he could, R.L.S. was off, on the train south, 'take me South where the air is as warm as milk', and south he went, as far away as he could, as far south as he could go, to Bournemouth, to the South of France, to his final home (and resting-place) in the South Seas, travelling, writing adventure stories, a complex, troubled bohemian who never quite escaped his roots, a writer whose fiction – for all its romantic gestures – is more interesting for its duality and its moral ambiguities. His final, unfinished novel, *Weir of Hermiston*, is set, significantly, not in the South Seas but back in Edinburgh, back in the Lowland hills, and centres on the conflict between a grim Scottish judge and his idealistic son. However far away he may travel, we realise, the son never quite escapes the father.

It is indeed a deep coastal shelf, a family.

Stevenson described his father as a man with a 'blended sternness and softness that is wholly Scottish and at first somewhat bewildering'. As far as I know, the full relevance of Stevenson's description of his father's nature has never been applied to Larkin's poem. Larkin clearly sets his second stanza against the background of Stevenson's, whose childhood experiences in soppy-stern 17 Heriot Row, with his tender nurse and his rigid father, are precisely echoed.

So much for the Stevenson background. When I first read the poem in 1974 I was shocked/amused by the ludicrous suggestion that parents deliberately handed on their genes and problems to their children, and then – with a spice of malice – sprinkled a few extra problems on top like muesli on the cornflakes. There I was, sitting next to my six-month-old daughter, wishing her a wonderful life and wondering how many of my features, how many of my characteristics and hang-ups she had inherited and would in time exhibit, while hearing at the same time my own father's voice reciting the Stevenson poem, a poem which he knew by heart.

My father taught me in class; I taught my son in class. I can see what I have inherited from my mother and father. I can see things my daughter and my son have inherited from my wife and me. Obviously it would be absurd to blame one's parents for everything, and it would be absurd for Larkin, even through a persona, to promote such an idea. And the whole point is that he does not. He sets up the controversial idea, indeed he seems to embrace it, as he so often does, only to knock it down. All we have to do is think the logic through. If we blame our parents not only for conceiving us but also for handing us all our problems, then it logically follows that our parents can just as readily blame *their* parents for everything, and we can all go on shifting the blame back one generation at a time, *ad infinitum*, *ad absurdum*.

So that won't do. Because if that *is* the case we might as well all opt out of the living business altogether and have no children. And if people have no children that is the end of the living business. ('The final negative,' as the Brazilian novelist Machado de Assis puts it, 'the final negative of this chapter of negatives: I had no progeny, I transmitted to no one the legacy of our misery.') Absurd. So, Larkin's poem ends by suggesting something very different from its meaning at first sight. Suffering and pain are part of the human condition; man is born to trouble as surely as the sparks fly upwards. We should, Larkin implies, stop blaming our parents for bequeathing us our real or grave or imagined problems, and start accepting responsibility for our own lives.

This Larkin technique – of catching his reader's attention by adopting a fashionable or cynical or modish attitude – and then leading the reader to an altogether deeper and more searching understanding is one which teachers and parents could well, in my view, adopt as a model. For example, many children are bored at school. Fact. It is hard for teachers to beat this boredom problem because it is part of adolescence. That is an Opinion which I would also claim as a Fact. Boredom, real or affected, is here to stay. The young are good at it. They want to be. They work on it. They polish it into a style. They give it the same attention as they give their hair, and that is pretty serious attention.

Given all this, it is better for teachers and parents to accept it as a starting point (which is not at all the same thing as giving in to it), and then to lead, to tease, to surprise, to deepen them out of it. That method works in many of Larkin's best poems, and it works better in class than high-minded idealism or shock-horror. 'Bored? Bored! I was never bored in my day.' Well, I was. Very bored. And I still do get very bored. Teachers and parents might do well quietly to ask themselves not only 'What was I like, really like, when I was young?' but also 'How much of me, however skilfully buried underneath, is still like that?'

You don't have to go in for cosy confessionals or unwelcome intimacy, which the young generally dislike. You don't have to tell your children or your pupils how it was for you, or all you did. But it is a good idea to have that film, directed by an active conscience, playing in the background.

37
Coming To Terms

It's not easy ending books, and it's not easy facing the end of a career. In art and in life the beginnings and the endings tend to be the most difficult; once you're launched, once you've set out on your journey, things often have their own momentum.

So, I am moving into the last chapter, in much the same way as I am coming up to my last year in the classroom. The last lap. The final timetable to check. And I have been trying to come to terms with it all, with a job which has excited and pushed me to my limits as a person. I have put what I think and believe about teaching into this book, and I have no plan to insult you all by coming up with a neat, oversimplified summary. That would only remind me of the thousands of essays I have marked which conclude with a re-statement of all I have just ploughed through. *I know you think that*, I feel like screaming, *I've just read it!*

So, what kind of ending is it to be? Centre stage in the spotlight, or slinking off with no one noticing until they notice – if they do – that you're not there?

Will it be *Goodbye, Mr Chips* or *Grange Hill, Hope and Glory* or *To Serve Them All My Days, The Browning Version* or

Dead Poets Society, or, if we're really going for the music, *Mr Holland's Opus* . . . If my life were a novel or a film, and I were a loved teacher, I might soon be walking into the school hall, with everyone standing and clapping, with the whole orchestra playing and me with a lump in my throat, with staff and governors and pupils past and present and from far and wide, and if I were a Mr Holland I would be asked to go up on stage, to take the baton and to conduct my very own composition, the very first full performance of my opus. (If my profession will not accept payment by results, it seems we will have to swallow payment by tears.)

No, really, but no. I mean it. I want to go quietly. Then open a bottle and sit and listen to some of my favourite jazz musicians, say Julian 'Cannonball' Adderley and Miles Davis playing 'Autumn Leaves' (recorded on 9 March 1958) or Coleman Hawkins encountering Ben Webster on 16 October 1957. What sounds, what style! Or we could listen to something you've brought round which you're dying to play me.

I don't want to say anything, if you don't mind, because I will be upset. The point is – and I would rather write than speak this – I did not stay in one school for so long because I wanted to serve it, or out of duty or from any sense of obligation. I am proud of the school, of course, but I stayed here because I enjoyed it. I am still here because I enjoy it. I have coached the 3rd XI in cricket for thirty-three years because I enjoy it. The same goes for the plays, for everything really. If I ever go to school feeling low in spirits, it does not take long for the teaching experience (in all its many unpredictable ways) to lift and to energise me.

Will I miss it? Of course I will. It is a community and a way of life as well as a daily, professional challenge. Of course I will miss it, I have had so many laughs. I cannot exaggerate how funny dealing with young people can be, and how much my colleagues and I laugh. Even on the grimmest days we enjoy a

hangman's humour; even on the rainiest days we wet ourselves. The English Department at Tonbridge, how could I
ever forget all that and all of them?

I hope, as a result of reading this book, that more parents
will teach their children, and will think about their own roles
in their children's education – and not just in the classroom.
I hope more teachers will stop apologising for the life they
have chosen. I hope more of my colleagues will find that elusive balance. I hope more of my pupils will come to love
books; and I hope that some of them will consider teaching as
a profession – a profession which, if not the noblest of them
all, is most certainly a noble one.

But it's time for me to move on. I have been saying for
years that I want to spend the rest of my life writing, rather
than trying to fit my writing into whatever time that has been
left from my teaching. No excuses from now on, nowhere to
hide. No more 'If only I didn't have this pile of marking . . .'
It'll be a matter of 'Just get on with it, Jonathan.

> – So, when the time comes, no regrets?
> – None.
> – You're sure of that?
> – I'm sure.
> – No doubts?
> – No doubts.
> – Seriously?
> – Seriously.
> – A final word?

Well . . . look . . . all right . . . OK. The best I can do is to
finish with some words, not my words, but words which have
long been glued to the inside of my classroom door. They can
say it for me, they're close to what I believe, and they say it so
much better than I can. As you know, I like to have little

things pinned up all around me, to keep me going, to lift my
sights, to inspire me and to reassure me about the things that
really matter. These words were written – appropriately
enough – by someone who, just over a hundred years ago, left
the school at which I am proud to teach.

> The people I most admire are those who are sensitive and
> want to create something or discover something, and do
> not see life in terms of power . . . They produce literature
> and art, or they do disinterested scientific research, or
> they may be what is called 'ordinary people', who are cre-
> ative in their private lives, bring up their children
> decently, or help their neighbours.
>
> I believe in the aristocracy of the sensitive, the consid-
> erate and the plucky. Its members are to be found in all
> nations and all classes, and all through the ages there is a
> secret understanding between them when they meet.
> They represent the true human condition. They are sensi-
> tive to others, as well as for themselves, they are
> considerate without being fussy, their pluck is not swanki-
> ness but the power to endure, and they can take a joke.

E. M. FORSTER (1879–1970), *What I Believe*